WORDS AROUND THE FONT

WORDS AROUND THE FONT

by

GAIL RAMSHAW

art by

LINDA EKSTROM

Liturgy Training Publications

With gratitude, sempervirent, to Gordon Lathrop

———————

Also in this series:

Words around the Fire
Reflections on the scripture readings of the Easter Vigil

Words around the Table
Reflections on the words and deeds of the Sunday Eucharist

Words That Sing
Reflections on Christian hymnody

The scripture pericopes contained herein are from the *Revised Standard Version Bible,* copyright © 1946, 1952, 1971 by the Division of Christian Education of the National Council of Churches of Christ in the U.S.A., as emended in the *Lectionary for the Christian People,* copyright © 1988 by Pueblo Publishing Company, Inc. Used with permission of The Liturgical Press. All rights reserved.

Words around the Font was designed by Jill Smith and typeset in Goudy by Jim Mellody-Pizzato. It was edited by Gabe Huck; the production editor was Deborah Bogaert. Printed by BookCrafters of Chelsea, Michigan.

Library of Congress Cataloging-in-Publications Data

Ramshaw, Gail, 1947-
    Words around the font / by Gail Ramshaw ; art by Linda Ekstrom.
      p. cm.
    ISBN 1-56854-063-9
    1. Catechumens—Prayer-books and devotions—English. 2. Baptism—Prayer-books and devotions—English. 3. Catholic Church—Prayer-books and devotions—English. I. Title.
BX2170.C38R35 1994
264'.020813–dc20
                                    94-24022
                                        CIP

CONTENTS

WAYS TO USE THIS BOOK

Spirituality

The close of the twentieth century has witnessed a fascination with "spirituality": week-long retreats, adult discussion groups, university courses, blank books designed for journaling, even chain bookstores pushing one kind of spirituality or another. Because a spirituality is a way of being religious, it is not surprising that in a religiously diverse culture the word connotes many different, sometimes antithetical, things.

Even within Christianity there are diverse spiritualities. A Franciscan spirituality sees life with the poor as the key to Christ and so to religious truth. An Ignatian spirituality stresses individual mental exercises as a method of identifying with Christ, a helpful technique for some types of minds, fruitless for others. Denominations historically have had distinctive spiritualities. A Lutheran spirituality proclaims a cross-centered theology with robust hymnody, while an Anglican spirituality expresses the incarnation in elegant ritual. In a Christian spirituality Christ is the center, but there are many different ways to see Christ.

Liturgical spirituality

This book is an exercise in "liturgical spirituality." In Christian liturgical spirituality, life in the spirit of Christ is sought through the rhythm, forms, words and melodies of the liturgy. The yearly, weekly and daily cycles of praise and prayer provide the materials for focus on Christ. To be religious in this way, we do the liturgy—we accomplish its actions, repeat its prayers, sing its songs, embrace its symbols—and, when the liturgy is over, we live as if it were still going on—in praise of God and in loving care for one another. Benedictine monasticism has modeled this Christian spirituality for centuries. Many church fathers wrote expositions of the liturgy. Many mystics experienced their ecstasies during or after worship. In our century, Romano Guardini wrote *Meditations before Mass*. From Mary's Magnificat and St. Benedict's community to Gertrude of Helfta and Thomas Merton, the idea is this: The way we are religious comes from the liturgy and goes back to the liturgy. We live the way we praise. Liturgical spirituality asks two questions: (1) What does the liturgy "say" that we mean, and (2) if we attend to this meaning, how will we live? Liturgical commentary seeks to assist in these questions and answers. These, we say, have been and ought still to be the meanings of the liturgy. This, we say, might be how we will live, if the liturgy is singing in our soul.

How to make use of this book

The books in this series of liturgical spirituality—*Words around the Fire, Words around the Table, Words around the Font,* even *Words That Sing*—could be used in many different contexts. Adult learners, whether a catechumenal group or a small evening discussion class, might read through the book together and discuss its implications. Individuals, whether reading by themselves in a daily devotional time or guided week by week with a spiritual director, might explore personal reactions to these meditations. The citations written in the margins provide suggestions for Bible study.

In *Words around the Font*, thirteen meditations are set out to accompany the catechumens on their way toward baptism. You may wish to read the table of contents at this point to understand the plan of this book. You will see, for example, that during the period of evangelization, we need to contemplate both divine perfection and human sin, the words of both Genesis 1 and Genesis 3. You may wish to have before you the church's baptismal texts as you use this book. (Roman Catholic texts can be found in the *Rite of Christian Initiation of Adults*; many Protestant churches include their baptismal text in the pew edition of their service book.)

These meditations also take into account the church's readings from scripture. Because the optimal time for baptismal catechesis is the lenten season, culminating in the Easter Vigil, the lenten readings for Cycle A are the biblical texts presented here. For example, during the period of instruction, we all hear the texts from John: the woman at the well, the man born blind and the raising of Lazarus. We all move together into the Triduum, with its foot-washing from John 11, and so on to baptism itself. This book connects the process of initiation with the annual liturgical journey to the Easter Vigil, because according to a liturgical spirituality, all baptized Christians recall each year their entry into the death and resurrection of Christ.

In *Words around the Font*, six elements play off one another. First is a biblical text. The texts were chosen because theologians, teachers and preachers describing baptism had recourse to these very texts throughout the centuries of the church. It is important to read the text first and to keep its images before you. Second is a quote from an ancient liturgical text or a selection from the writings of the church fathers or mothers. These quotes were chosen because they use the biblical texts in a distinctive way. Liturgical spirituality discovers that the great teachers of the faith throw interesting light on our path. Third is the text of the meditation itself. These meditations bring together various biblical references, the testimony of the saints and contemporary cultural meaning in a reflection on the meaning of the liturgy. Fourth is a prayer, meant more for individual meditation than for corporate worship. Perhaps these prayers will inspire you or your group toward improvised prayer. Fifth is a set of questions. These questions are meant not to evoke certain correct answers but rather to encourage "liturgical" thinking among us. Lastly, art ties together all the pieces. Like fancy stitching in a crazy quilt, the art holds the oddly shaped fabrics side by side so that the different designs and textures are juxtaposed with no holes between them.

The liturgy is such a quilt—one swatch from an old linen tablecloth, one from grandma's flowered housedress, one from grandpa's plaid shirt. Liturgical spirituality is such a quilt. Wrap yourself up in it. It is wondrously warm in a shivering world.

INTRODUCTION

"Tell me, Nicodemus, how was Isaac begotten?"

JOHN CHRYSOSTOM

Remembering Isaac

In 389, to teach the meaning of baptism, John Chrysostom, the bishop of Constantinople famed for his eloquent sermons, preached 88 homiles on the gospel of John. Imagining that Nicodemus, who came to Jesus by night to be instructed in the faith, was a cate-chumen sitting before him, Chrysostom recalled the story of Isaac to illustrate birth from God. Isaac, the son of Sarah and Abraham, was born through the usual birth process; but Sarah, 90 years old at the time of his birth, conceived—as did many biblical women—beyond nature. Like Isaac's birth, our birth in God is both through

John 3:1–21

Genesis 18:9–15

nature and beyond nature, a way we can explain and a way we cannot.

Some Christians have stressed the first. For them, baptism is a human ritual which, just as we see in numerous other religions, initiates the individual into the life of the community. After a lengthy process of preparation, the believing adult abandons an old set of values and volunteers to join a new family, adopting its members as sisters and brothers. The procession to the riverside is a victorious parade from the battlefield to the new city.

But other Christians have taught the second: Baptism is nothing less than a miracle, an instance of divine intervention, a piece of Christ's resurrection, the sixth day of creation repeated. The blue baby, gasping between death and life, is nearly nothing; yet three drops of water on its head by the harried Christian nurse, and before us lies a saint of God.

Guess what: It's the same baptism. It's two enactments of the one truth. Isaac is born to a married couple; Isaac is born of a post-menopausal woman. The eager adult runs forward to join the community's hold on divine grace, while God's mercy in the church enfolds the dying infant.

One baptism

Like Chrysostom, we probe the meaning of baptism. Around the font are heard many words, mostly biblical phrases, each illuminating part of the Christian mystery of entrance into grace. This book will reflect on some of these words, their place in the ritual, their biblical resonances, the ways the church fathers and mothers taught them and their possible meanings for our time. Because *Exodus 24:1–4* in both Jewish and Christian numerology twelve is a sign of comple- *Revelation 21:10–14* tion, we will consider thirteen phrases—for our list can never be complete; there are always more ways to say God's grace. To accompany the catechumens, these reflections are organized according to the process of the Rite of Christian Initiation of Adults. But references to the RCIA will not be overt, lest the book become bothersome for other users, the old-timers who with Martin Luther know that each day for each Christian is a "creeping back to baptism."

In Assy, France, is a church famed for its twentieth century art. Off the nave is a baptistry graced with a magnificent depiction of the exodus, created by Marc Chagall. Moses is holding back Pharaoh and his chariots; an angel is leading the people safely across the sea toward the cross of Christ. It is a stunning piece, with the Jewish artist serving the Christian telling the Jewish story. The Chagall, nearly overwhelming the visitor with its symbolic power, dwarfs a singularly unimpressive font, a small bowl on a pedestal designed for cute infants in white ruffles. The Exodus painting tells of ancient times, the violent destruction of evil, glorious visions from God and the mystery of the cross. The font tells of a 1950s French baby being christened. Guess what: It's the same baptism.

Exodus 14:26–30

Let's go, Nicodemus, to find some answers to how these things can be.

THE IMAGE OF GOD

In the beginning God created the heavens and the earth. The earth was without form and void, and darkness was upon the face of the deep; and the Spirit of God was moving over the face of the waters.

And God said, "Let there be light"; and there was light. And God saw that the light was good; and God separated the light from the darkness. God called the light Day, and the darkness God called Night. And there was even-ing and there was morning, one day.

And God said, "Let there be a firmament in the midst of the waters, and let it separate the waters from the waters." And God made the firmament and separated the waters which were under the firmament from the waters which were above the firmament. And it was so. And God called the firmament Heaven. And there was evening and there was morning, a second day.

And God said, "Let the waters under the heavens be gathered together into one place, and let the dry land appear." And it was so. God called the dry land Earth, and the waters that were gathered together God called Seas. And God saw that it was good. And God said, "Let the earth put forth vegetation, plants yielding seed, and fruit trees bearing fruit in which is their seed, each according to its kind, upon the earth." And it was so. The earth brought forth

vegetation, plants yielding seed according to their own kinds, and trees bearing fruit in which is their seed, each according to its kind. And God saw that it was good. And there was evening and there was morning, a third day.

And God said, "Let there be lights in the firmament of the heavens to separate the day from the night; and let them be for signs and for seasons and for days and years, and let them be lights in the firmament of the heavens to give light upon the earth." And it was so. And God made the two great lights, the greater light to rule the day, and the lesser light to rule the night; God made the stars also. And God set them in the firmament of the heavens to give light upon the earth, to rule over the day and night, and to separate the light from the darkness. And God saw that it was good. And there was evening and there was morning, a fourth day.

And God said, "Let the waters bring forth swarms of living creatures, and let birds fly above the earth across the firmament of the heavens." So God created the great sea monsters and every living creature that moves, with which the waters swarm, according to their kinds, and every winged bird according to its kind. And God saw that it was good. And God blessed them, saying, "Be fruitful and multiply and fill the waters in the seas, and let birds multiply on the earth." And there was evening and there was morning, a fifth day.

And God said, "Let the earth bring forth living creatures according to their kinds: cattle and creeping things and beasts of the earth according to their kinds." And it was so. And God made the beasts of the earth according to their kinds and the cattle according to their kinds, and everything that creeps upon the ground according to its kind. And God saw that it was good.

Then God said, "Let us make humankind in our image, after our likeness; and let them have dominion over the fish of the sea, and over the birds of the air, and over the cattle, and over all the earth, and over every creeping thing that creeps upon the earth." So God created humankind in the divine image; in the image of God humankind was created; male and female God created them. And God blessed them, and God said to them, "Be fruitful and multiply, and fill the earth and subdue it; and have dominion over the fish of the sea and over the birds of the air and over every living thing that moves upon the earth." And God said, "Behold, I have given you every plant yielding seed which is upon the face of all the earth, and every tree with seed in its fruit; you shall have them for food. And to every beast of the earth, and to every bird of the air, and to everything that creeps on the earth, everything that has the breath of life, I have given every green plant for food." And it was so. And God saw everything that had been made, and behold, it was very good. And there was evening and there was morning, a sixth day.

Thus the heavens and the earth were finished, and all the host of them. And on the seventh day God finished the work which had been done, and God rested on the seventh day from all the work which God had done. So God blessed the seventh day and hallowed it, because on it God rested from all the work which God had done in creation.

> # "May they receive the likeness of God."
>
> ### THE AMBROSIAN LITURGY

In the beginning

As people begin to ask who they are, they narrate their stories of origin. Who are my parents? Where did my ancestors live? Tell me the tale of the first human beings. To navigate our seas, to make today's decisions, to sign up for baptism, I want to know where I began and what the journey thus far has been.

There's a world of cosmogonies out there. The Babylonian Enuma Elish says that the creator Marduk, having vanquished the evil monster Tiamat, used the blood of her lover Kinga to fashion human beings. The Melanesian story says that Qat fashioned human beings from wood and brought them to dancing life by playing on his drums. The Hindus push their four castes all the way back to creation, for each lower caste derived from a lower part of Parusha's body. According to a Chinese tale, the creator god P'an Ku turns into the world, and humankind emerges from his body lice. According to an ancient Egyptian version, the creator Re made us out of his tears.

Genesis 1

Christians have two creation stories, two quite different tales of how humans came to be. But let us begin at the beginning and tell the first story first. Genesis 1 narrates an idyllic cosmogony. Lest you doubt the existence of a deity, the story begins all life with God. Lest you dread a chaotic and unfocused universe, the story details a masterful flowering of the earth and its surroundings, with no second thoughts, no errors, no stray pieces falling off the edge. Lest you despair that pernicious time is defeating you, the story assures you that God, when inventing human time, designed a weekly gift of rest. Lest you sense terrors lurking around the corner and under the waters, the story assigns even the sea monsters their appointed place, under human care and concern. And when you weary that so many civilizations oppress women, Genesis 1 surprises you with equal males and females, created with the joy of sex. Divine providence, divine beneficence: There is no evil, all is very good.

Genesis 1:27   Genesis 1 tells us that we are created in the image of God, an enigmatic phrase which unfortunately its author neglected to define. Christians particularly, as they have prepared themselves and others for baptism, have been fascinated by this phrase and over the centuries have suggested a great variety of meanings for this similarity between the divine and the human. The Greek philosophical tradition suggested to early theologians that because God is total rationality, the image of God is human reason, and those people with more reasoning capability (who they assumed were males) had more of the image than others. Augustine ventured that the image was triune: human memory, understanding and will. Martin Luther taught that the image was our primordial orientation toward God; John Calvin, our paradisal moral perfection. Modern critics suggest it probably originally meant that humans represented divine royalty, or even that humans, like the deity, walked upright. When in Genesis 5:2 Adam becomes father to a son "in his likeness, according to his image," the words suggest physical similarity. Yet Jewish and Christian teachers have pooh-poohed that:

Surely the human being does not look like the incorporeal God. Perhaps, as Karl Barth imagined, it is gender distinction with its properly ordered male superiority; perhaps, as many teach today, it means the absolute opposite, gender parity; perhaps, as ecofeminists suggest, the divine image is care for the universe.

Ah, do you see what is happening? There is no clarity about what the phrase meant to its originators or to its editors, or what it ought to mean for contemporary Christians. So without realizing what we are doing, we focus on what we imagine is the highest human good—rationality or moral perfection or male supremacy or gender equality—and define the God of Genesis 1 accordingly, so that we become recipients from God of this most prized possession. Are you surprised that for Paul Ricoeur, who writes about symbolic language, the divine image is symbol-making capability? The serpent is swallowing its tail.

Still probing

Perhaps Christians can do no more with this elusive "divine image." Perhaps none of us can get enough beyond ourselves to imagine not merely our highest values, but the divine life. Perhaps my offering yet another interpretation is no more than my personal value projected into the sky, my meditation disturbed by Freud's cynical laughter.

But we can't lay Genesis 1 down. Its perfection beckons us, its mystery attracts us back to the beneficent origin of all. If this is who I am, I'd better know about it. For if it were true, if humans were, are and can be in the divine image, my journey will be different than if not.

The triune image

So here's another try. Too often we think of God as one great being in the sky. For Christians, however, God is triune, God connected, intertwined, permeating. God is not distant, retired or angry, but continuously creating and cradling the world. God is not alien to the human race but in Jesus joined it, the divine life intertwined with folk like Mary Magdalene and Malchus. God is not stuck in the historic Christ but permeates the community even today, turning human spirit into divine spirit for the good of the universe.

Luke 8:1–2
John 18:10–11

And if that's the triune God, then we in that divine image are connected to, intertwined with, and permeating the created order and its human inhabitants. For contemporary Americans parading our individuality, such blimps that our hot air prevents us from close contact with others, recognizing and claiming this image of God is the single most significant of our life passages. The threefold life of baptism is not a club beating us up (So what happened to your moral perfection, you rotten sinner?!) but a gift of communion, a gold ring signifying our marriage to the whole earth and its peoples, the end of isolation, the beginning of what life is meant to be.

Martin Luther teaches us to call Genesis 1 "gospel," the good news that by the mercy of God all is very good. Like the urchins in a Charles Dickens novel who discover that they are actually the children of royalty, we are pulled out of our gutter by this newfound autobiography. The divine image calls us to rest in God's arms even when the sea monster is readying for the attack and to welcome human interaction as the context within which we thrive.

All over Europe and Africa archeologists are excavating ancient baptistries, discovering that far from fingerbowls, the place of baptism in many cities was an octagonal in-ground pool. In one such pool in Milan, Ambrose baptized Augustine, the legend recording that as they came out from the pool, arm in arm, bound together to Christ, to one another and to believers of all time, they composed the hymn we know as the Te Deum on the spot. A tenth-century manuscript of the baptismal liturgy as practiced in Milan includes the petition, "May they receive the likeness of God." I like to think of Augustine there in Milan receiving that likeness and contemplating it so unendingly that the likeness poured out in all his praise of the Trinity.

We had this likeness at our beginning. It is our mission to uncover it; yet we discover it less like buried treasure than like a surprise bequest. The gift is there before we have finished digging, already in our lap just as we were getting on our feet to start searching. It will of course take a lifetime to realize this image, to shape our individuality by its threefold liveliness, but at least in baptism, we have begun.

William Faulkner once quipped, "I tell the truth. When I need a fact, I make it up." List what is true in Genesis 1.

What distinguishes me from my cat?

Compare images of the Trinity.

What do you imagine "in God's image" to mean?

O living God,

connect us to yourself;

entwine us with each other and all the world you made;

permeate us with your Spirit,

that we may live as your image,

through Christ, the living one.

I HID MYSELF

GENESIS 2:4b — 3:24

In the day that the LORD God made
the earth and the heavens, when no plant
of the field was yet in the earth and
no herb of the field had yet sprung up—
for the LORD God had not caused it to
rain upon the earth, and there was no
one to till the ground; but a mist went up
from the earth and watered the whole
face of the ground—then the LORD God
formed a man of dust from the ground,
and breathed into his nostrils the breath
of life; and the man became a living
being. And the LORD God planted a
garden in Eden, in the east, and there the
LORD God put the man who had been
made. And out of the ground the LORD
God made to grow every tree that is
pleasant to the sight and good for food,
the tree of life also in the midst of the
garden, and the tree of knowledge of good
and evil.

A river flowed out of Eden to water
the garden, and there it divided and
became four rivers. The name of the first
is Pishon; it is the one which flows
around the whole land of Havilah, where
there is gold; and the gold of that land
is good; bdellium and onyx stone are there.
The name of the second river is Gihon;
it is the one which flows around the
whole land of Cush. And the name of
the third river is Tigris, which flows
east of Assyria. And the fourth river is
the Euphrates.

The LORD God took the man and
put him in the garden of Eden to till it
and keep it. And the LORD God
commanded the man, saying, "You
may freely eat of every tree of the garden;
but of the tree of knowledge of good
and evil you shall not eat, for in the day
that you eat of it you shall die."

The LORD God said, "It is not good
that the man should be alone; I will make
him a companion fit for him" So out
of the ground the LORD God formed
every beast of the field and every bird of
the air, and brought them to the man
to see what he would call them; and
whatever the man called every living
creature, that was its name. The
man gave names to all cattle, and to the
birds of the air, and to every beast of
the field; but for the man there was not
found a companion fit for him. So
the LORD God caused a deep sleep to fall
upon the man, and while he slept took
one of his ribs and closed up its place with
flesh; and the rib which the LORD
God had taken from the man, the LORD
God made into a woman and brought
her to the man. Then the man said,

> "This at last is bone of my bones
> and flesh of my flesh;
> she shall be called a woman,
> because she was taken out of
> a man."

*Therefore a man leaves his father
and his mother and cleaves to his wife,
and they become one flesh.*

*And they both, the man and his wife,
were naked, and were not ashamed.*

*Now the serpent was more subtle
than any other wild creature that the
LORD God had made. The serpent said
to the woman, "Did God say, 'You shall
not eat of any tree of the garden'?"
And the woman said to the serpent, "We
may eat of the fruit of the trees of the
garden; but God said, 'You shall not eat
of the fruit of the tree which is in the
midst of the garden, neither shall you
touch it, lest you die.'" But the serpent
said to the woman, "You will not die.
For God knows that when you eat of it
your eyes will be opened, and you
will be like God, knowing good and
evil." So when the woman saw that the
tree was good for food, and that it was a
delight to the eyes, and that the tree
was to be desired to make one wise, she
took of its fruit and ate; and she also
gave some to her husband, and he
ate. Then the eyes of both were opened,
and they knew that they were naked;
and they sewed fig leaves together and
made themselves aprons.*

*And they heard the sound of the
LORD God walking in the garden in the
cool of the day, and the man and his
wife hid themselves. But the LORD God
called to the man, and said to him,
"Where are you?" And he said, "I heard
the sound of you in the garden, and*

*I was afraid, because I was naked; and I
hid myself." God said, "Who told you
that you were naked? Have you eaten of
the tree of which I commanded you not
to eat?" The man said, "The woman
whom you gave to be with me, she gave
me fruit of the tree, and I ate." Then
the LORD God said to the woman,
"What is this that you have done?" The
woman said, "The serpent beguiled
me, and I ate." The LORD God said to
the serpent,*

"Because you have done this,
cursed are you above all cattle,
and above all wild animals;
upon your belly you shall go,
and dust you shall eat
all the days of your life.
I will put enmity between you and
the woman,
and between your offspring and
her offspring;
her offspring shall bruise your head,
and you shall bruise his heel."

To the woman God said,

"I will greatly multiply your pain in
childbearing;
in pain you shall bring forth
children,
yet your desire shall be for your
husband,
and he shall rule over you."

And to Adam God said,

"Because you have listened to the
voice of your wife,
and have eaten of the tree
of which I commanded you,

'You shall not eat of it,'
cursed is the ground because of you;
   in toil you shall eat of it all the
      days of your life;
thorns and thistles it shall bring forth
      to you;
   and you shall eat the plants of
      the field.
In the sweat of your face
   you shall eat bread
till you return to the ground,
   for out of it you were taken;
you are dust,
   and to dust you shall return."

The man called his wife's name Eve,
because she was the mother of all living.

And the LORD God made for Adam
and for his wife garments of skins, and
clothed them.

Then the LORD God said, "Behold,
the man has become like one of us,
knowing good and evil; and now, lest he
put forth his hand and take also of the
tree of life, and eat, and live for ever" —
therefore the LORD God sent him forth
from the garden of Eden, to till the
ground from which he was taken. The
LORD God drove out the man, and
placed at the east of the garden of Eden
the cherubim, and a flaming sword which
turned every way, to guard the way to
the tree of life.

> **"You are absolute directness and I am terrible twistedness."**
>
> CATHERINE OF SIENA

A *twisting tale*

In Genesis 1 is divine artistry, universal clarity and human perfection. The comforting directness of the poem's rondo-like repetition— "and God saw that it was good"—conveys the elegance of the creation and God's straightforward intent for its human creatures. But the Bible is not naive: The sleek and wondrous tale of Genesis 1 crashes into Genesis 2–3, the second and rather more twisted story of our creation.

Even the first sentence of the second story is convoluted: no plants yet, no rain, but some dew, in a sentence grammatically malformed. The order of this story is illogical. Androcentric through and through, Genesis 2 has the male created first. Next comes a garden, presumably to provide food. Mixed in with the four rivers, essential for human life, is the location of gold, a hint of the distorted values of the civilization that is coming round the bend. The man is lonely. God appears something of a novice, trying this, trying that. Here, man, here's a dog! Do you prefer a cat? The man is still lonely, at work, naming the animals. The deity finally gets it right, at least from a man's point of view: From a curved rib comes the stuff for a woman, the companion he desires, as if what the man requires is only part of himself spruced up a bit.

Into this sketchy story—what are they eating? how long is this taking? are the animals wild? do all the animals talk?—a serpent twists itself through the grass. The serpent makes a sketchy promise. Yes, their eyes will be open. They will indeed be like the Jewish God, distinguishing good from evil. But the serpent hides the rest of the future, neglecting to warn them about the misery of being fully human: the cataclysmic battle between good and evil, the pain of childbirth, the sorrows of sexual inequality, the oppression within human society, the unending toil to provide food and shelter, the inevitability of death. The partial story sounded just fine, but soon the man and the woman are hiding in the bushes, contorting their bodies behind a tree, a rock, a St. Bernard, anything, to avoid the direct gaze of God.

Hiding from the story

Granting the story's archaic worldview, its childish ordering of events, its anthropomorphic depiction of God and its repellent misogyny, many contemporary Christians have laid it aside as too untrue for continued consideration. Surely this tale is too demeaning, too depressing: I am not to blame for eating the fruit! What's wrong with eating the fruit anyway? Others, completely misinterpreting what Augustine meant by "original sin," use the story to "prove" that while there is some sin around, it is surely not our own most grevious fault. It is Adam's and Eve's fault instead, as if the story wishes to instruct us only in the human propensity for blaming the snake, each other, anybody but ourselves.

I hide from the exposure of this twisted story, denying its piercing truth, a truth deeper than its cosmology and misogyny. I try to avoid this unpleasant realization that I twist God's creation out of shape. I deny the paradox of being human: that we, like God, are to distinguish good from evil as we, like all creatures, live toward certain death. I set up a reverse fun-house mirror in my room, and it makes perfectly straight what Genesis 2–3 says I twisted. Why, now I look just fine. Hiding from this story requires retreating far enough that I don't get disturbed by the voice of God. Did you hear someone calling? No, it was just the wind rustling through the leaves of the tree of knowledge of good and evil. But where in the world are my clothes?

I myself

The tree I hide behind is too stunted to shield us both, and so what was made to be connected, intertwined and permeating must now be alone. I myself attend to my own protection; I myself must cover my nakedness. I blame even the one I love the most: Surely it is your fault! I fly away from the spiraling story of Genesis 1, becoming a black hole out by myself somewhere. Or I can hardly breathe, closed up in this box by myself. Where in the world is someone else?

Like Catherine

Catherine of Siena was a fourteenth century mystic famous for poetic prayers, religious ecstasy, political and ecclesiastical activism, for living in most ways outside of social expectations. Catherine knew about such hiding, and she feared the strangulation of the self. We need not, as did Catherine, twist ouselves even worse into convoluted wrecks, willing ourselves into agony, fasting ourselves to death. In her prayers is a self-loathing that repels us, but Catherine knew distortion when she saw it, and she bravely named it between her prayers of ecstasy. Priests, cut it out! Pope, go home! Catherine, you yourself are twisted, she railed, crying out for the directness of Genesis 1 in a church and world gone haywire. All that we find alien in Catherine, a semi-balanced medieval vision-ary, can give way before her gift to us: She believed Genesis 2–3.

The second truth

To be evangelized is to hear the good news. Yes, Genesis 1 is good news, the gospel of the mercy of God. But paradoxically there is good news also in Genesis 2–3, the tale of divine perfection becom-ing twisted. It is the good news of real truth, which we must come to know, to admit, to see in the mirror each morning and in the hole dug in the cemetery; for, as the serpent's ploy should teach us, no news which is not all the news can finally be good.

This news is good because it throws us out from behind the tree of the knowledge of good and evil, where we were trying to hide, and into the light of day one of creation. Genesis 2–3 forces us back to Genesis 1. The light from the cherubim's flaming sword, the blinding glare of the truth of twistedness, turns us back to God's creation of light, the first goodness in which all dark-ness was cut open by merciful light. Both stories of our creation call us back to God.

What is your least favorite part of Genesis 2:4b—3:24?

What are all the reasons we wear clothes?

What do we make of the "saintliness" of persons like Catherine of Siena?

What about the tree of life?

I hide,

O God,

undressed, alone.

Show me a rock to hide behind,

1 Corinthians 10:4 make the rock Christ,

your own body on this earth.

SIGNED WITH THE CROSS

MARK 4:35 – 41

On that day, when evening had come, Jesus said to the disciples, "Let us go across to the other side." And leaving the crowd, they took him with them in the boat, just as he was. And other boats were with him. And a great storm of wind arose, and the waves beat into the boat, so that the boat was already filling. But Jesus was in the stern, asleep on the cushions; and they woke him and said to him, "Teacher, do you not care if we perish?" And Jesus awoke and rebuked the wind, and said to the sea, "Peace! Be still." And the wind ceased, and there was a great calm. Jesus said to them, "Why are you afraid? Have you no faith?" And they were filled with awe, and said to one another, "Who then is this, that even wind and sea obey him?"

> "They set sail with the cross for their mast."

GALLICAN RITE

Christians mark their lives with the cross. Parents trace a cross on their children's foreheads in the morning before school; on Epiphany, some folks still take chalk to mark their front doors with the new year and a cross; there are crosses on rings, crosses on chains, crosses as gravemarkers. In the eighteenth century, when the painted caves of France were rediscovered, some Christian was upset enough by the mysterious power of the prehistoric art to carve a cross and an IHS on top of a painted mammoth, as if the ancient religion still needed conquering. Legend says that only by holding up a cross can you keep the vampires away. It begins even before baptism, when the catechumens have their fore-head, ears, eyes, lips, heart, shoulders, hands and feet signed with the cross. In baptism we take on the cross because the cross took us on.

What's the cross about?

But what does it mean to mark our lives with an instrument of exe-cution? How do we pour significance for life out of a representation of death? The middle ages tried with the theory of substitutionary atonement: God was required to punish someone for sin and so appointed "his Son" as the victim. The cross was a sign of punishment meted out and of our debt to the one executed for us. Not an attractive theory, say many contemporary people, for whom this sounds more like child abuse than divine anything.

The New Testament phrase "Take up the cross" provided the basis for another influential interpretation. Life is suffering, say these Buddha-like Christians; the suffering that Christ experienced on Good Friday is a paradigm of our own suffering; because it is willingly accepted, it is somehow salvific. For Christians unable to change the circumstances of their lives, perhaps the acceptance of life as a private cross kept the despairing from suicide. But this theory also strikes many contemporary people as deficient.

Matthew 10:38

The task is to allow the cross to say all that it can, to be a symbolic representation of volumes of theological theories and myriad human stories. The simple "T" must encompass not only those tortured saints but also the contented, fruitful life of my old grandmother. Perhaps "the cross" means something somewhat different for each human who dons it, each member of Christ's body bearing it in a unique way. Like "the dominion of God" in the parables of Jesus in Mark 4, "the cross" eludes our understanding, and even though the disciples received an explanation, Mark attests that they didn't understand it at all.

Matthew 4:1–34

A liturgical metaphor

The liturgical speech of the church in Rome was succinct court address: You were to name the emperor, praise the emperor, state your request, and clear out of the throneroom. By contrast, the early liturgies in far-off Gaul were characterized by lush rhetoric, piles of images and interwined phrases. It is not surprising that images to illumine the cross are found in the old Gallican rites. It is as if these images are branches full of flowers or fruits or nuts which were lopped off the tree of life. In Normandy, France, town squares are still marked with statuary called calvaries, in which Christ's cross is depicted as a tree with all branches but the crossbeam broken off. Rereading the old Gallican rites is like finding a branch or two lying around near the trunk of the tree of life.

"They set sail with the cross for their mast," said the presider blessing a Gallican font. Probably echoing ancient cosmogonic myths of the wild sea monster being torn apart, or at least tamed, by the conquering deity, the scriptures bring us repeated images of crossing over the waters. In Genesis 1, God tames the watery chaos; the Israelites cross over the sea to escape death; Joshua leads the tribes over the Jordan to claim the promised land; Jonah discovers that God has charge over even the distant ocean; and the three synoptic gospels tell of Jesus stilling the storm, like the eternal God able to calm winds and to level waves. Early Christians adopted the metaphor of the ship for the church, which with the might of Christ could navigate life's stormiest seas. And the mast of the ship is the cross.

Gen 1:2

Ex 14:22

Joshua 3:15–16

Jonah 2:5–6

Mk 4:35–41

Such a ship!

With the sheets snapping in the wind and the deck pitching on the waves, the ship sets sail. Perhaps we'll see the mer-people that Lucy saw as she sailed to the edge of Narnia's world.

Perhaps we'll find the lost island of Atlantis, or some empty land ours for the taking rather than for the stealing. Perhaps we'll reflect on deep and wondrous ideas as we gaze out toward a horizon of yet more water. With Christ as the mast, the Spirit's wind will blow into full sails, and off we go toward the rainbow.

But perhaps not. Buoyed up by centuries of adventurous tales, we naively exaggerate the joys of such a voyage. We know from diaries that every league on a sailing ship was precarious. When there wasn't a storm to fear, there was mutany to avoid or—hey!— rats: Henry Muhlenberg, a Lutheran missionary sailing to colonial America in the early eighteenth century, recorded that because the crew lost their course and ran out of fresh water, the thirsty rats would lick the sweat off his face as he tried to sleep at night. And there was always the possibility of that greatest of disasters, a lightning strike destroying the mast.

In Mark 4, Jesus stills the storm, just as God could still the storms of Job's life and poetry. Of course, when we mark our lives with the cross, or sail with the cross as our mast, what we mean is that we mark our lives with Christ: for we sail with Christ as our mast. And here is yet another famous theory of how "the cross" saves: in the death of Christ, God takes on death and conquers it. The storm and its chaos are terrifying, malevolent. But Christ rests in the boat and rises to reprimand the wind and waves. He stands inside the storm and pacifies it, transforming its destructive power into a breath-taking sunset.

Job 38:1—42:6

I'm glad to read the instruction, "One who dies during the catechumenate receives a Christian burial." Once you sign on to this crew, you have the rights and privileges thereto appertaining (such as they are!)—the right to stand at the foot of the cross and the privilege of wearing it on your forehead.

What is your favorite depiction of the cross? Why? Is it similar to or different from the cross you knew as a child?

How has your life in the church been a grand adventure?

How has your life in the church been a sad disappointment?

Have you planned your funeral yet?

O unspeakable God,

we cannot say all your providence,

but only trace a cross instead.

May it be our spar,

catching your Spirit

Psalm 74:14 and triumphing over the sea monsters,

enabling our journey toward you.

REJECTING THE DEMONS

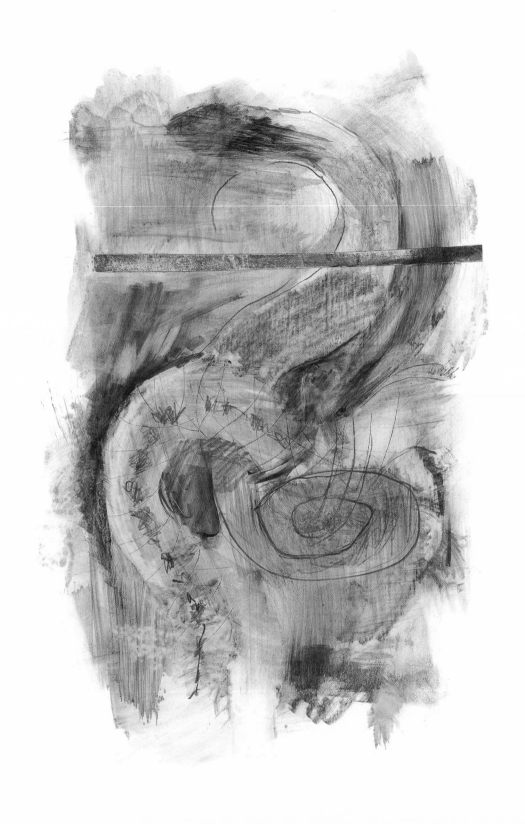

MARK 1:9 – 15

In those days Jesus came from Nazareth of Galilee and was baptized by John in the Jordan. And coming up out of the water, immediately Jesus saw the heavens opened and the Spirit descending upon him like a dove; and a voice came from heaven, "You are my Son, the beloved one; with you I am well pleased."

The Spirit immediately drove Jesus out into the wilderness.

And Jesus was in the wilderness forty days, tempted by Satan, and was with the wild beasts; and the angels ministered to him.

Now after John was arrested Jesus came into Galilee, preaching the gospel of God, and saying, "The time is fulfilled, and the dominion of God is at hand; repent, and believe in the gospel."

> "At the foot of the ladder lay a dragon of enormous size. Using it as my first step, I trod on its head and went up."

P E R P E T U A

A conversation with Quakers

Sometimes it seems as if William Penn's Quakerism is more alive than ever, increasingly marking the United States. The Quakers of Pennsylvania, in contrast to the stricter Protestant immigrants of New England, asserted that the Inner Light, the personal experience of God in the individual soul, is within every human person. People are basically good, because God lives within. Quakers do not write much about sin, which they see as resulting from our neglect of the Inner Light. There is much injustice in the world, but the divine Spirit within will encourage us to moral lives and social reform. Men and women are equal, and traditional hierarchies are to give way to a friendly egalitarianism. God in the inner soul makes unnecessary the church's authority, clergy and sacraments. Doesn't this sound like the popular American way? People are equal, people are good, God resides in each individual soul, and the trappings of religion are more harm than good.

Christian baptism must debate with this Quaker sensibility. Classical baptismal theology teaches that what naturally resides in "the soul," whatever we mean by that word, is the human self, which is more or less open to God's revelation. The revelation comes by grace, perhaps through many vehicles, but surely through the church's community, the word, and the sacraments. Evil is not merely the result of neglecting the Inner Light. Evil is a raging power, menacing, subtle, guileful and beguiling, daily at work to rot from within and to enslave from without. Some blame Eve, some blame patriarchy; but much more insidious than a single cause could effect, evil is an inexplicable multi-directional force, never at rest, as close as one's heart. If I imagine that evil can be neutralized in a 12-step program, my very naivete is an example of the phenomenon we call evil.

Is it a serpent?

People gave this evil a form so that they could recognize its malignant might, tell the tales of its malevolence and draw its outlines as a warning for the children. In the mythological system behind and in the Jewish and Christian stories, evil took the shape of a great serpent. Whether it was the sea monster Tiamat whom Marduk conquered, the dragon that the archangel Michael hurled from heaven, the serpent in Eden or the snakes that St. Patrick destroyed in Ireland, the scaley creatures were vanquished by the divinely-assisted hero. When in the year 203 the African woman Perpetua was imprisoned for espousing the cause of Christ, she recorded her visions of what the Christian faith was like. With martrydom by the beasts in the arena awaiting her, she saw life as a ladder to God and wrote, "At the foot of the ladder lay a dragon

Revelation 12:7–13

of enormous size. Using it as my first step, I trod on its head and went up." Dragons are nothing to Perpetua, to St. George, or to the baptized.

Recent scholarship demonstrates that in a yet more ancient symbol system, the serpent was the sign of female procreative power. In some stories she guarded the roots of the world tree, and in others she typified the wisdom of the oracle, for the periodic shedding of her skin was an image of the menstrual flow and everlasting life. Both layers of serpent imagery are found in the odd *Numbers 21:4–9* narrative in Numbers 21, in which evil fiery serpents are killing the Israelites; but by reverencing a bronze serpent erected on a pole, the people are healed. As with many metaphors, serpents have meant opposite things: The sea, for example, is honored as the womb of all life and dreaded as the occasion of uncontrollable death.

Is it the devil?

A second mythological image grew up alongside the serpent. In God's court up in heaven was a troublemaker who goaded God about what was right and wrong and accused human beings before the divine throne. According to the book of Job, the satan was *Job 2:1–18* God's designated tempter, an evil Pied Piper diverting those who were striving to live the moral life. Like the Norse god Loki, the satan caused endless mischief. Perhaps from their Zoroastrian neighbors the Jews came to aggrandize this satan into a devil, a primordial power nearly equal to God. By the time of Jesus, *Luke 10:17–20* Satan was understood as a supernatural champion of evil, responsible for the world's sin and misery, whom God must finally conquer at the end of time. This figure lives on in the liturgy, when for example the baptismal candidate renounces Satan, sometimes termed "the father of sin and prince of darkness"—male monarchical imagery having replaced the older female imagery of the great sea monster herself.

Is it both?

Our religious tradition equated the serpent with Satan. Students are always surprised to discover that Genesis 3 does not identify the talking snake as the devil, so closely have these two strands been woven together in the Christian imagination. In the bizarre fantasy of Revelation the single enemy of the faithful is "the dragon, that ancient serpent, who is the devil and Satan," the identification written as if the visionary is providing a thesaurus entry on "evil." Each image provides some facet of the reality of evil: There is the fire-breathing beast, the snake slithering through our backyard, the shadow side of God's reign, the major general of the maurading army.

Revelation 12:9

Is it demons?

The liturgy mythologizes evil in yet another way. Before baptism takes place, the demons must be rejected. The language of demonology suggests that we contend not against a single supernatural being residing in the earth's core but against innumerable and inexhaustible goads against God. All those interior proddings toward rotten behavior, all the external assaults on health and community, the whisper in my head advising that it's not my problem, the arrogance festering into an international crisis: these are demons all. This imagery is central to the synoptic gospels, in which Christ's casting out of demons is prelude to his final triumph over death. When Jesus enters through the world's doors, the demons are forced out the windows. Jesus appears, is baptized, calls a few disciples and commences his work by casting out a demon who recognizes him—and all in the first half of the first chapter of Mark.

What is it?

Contemporary Christians may find themselves using all of these images. Wicked dragons inhabit even new fairy tales; many believers find the existence of the devil a helpful idea; and the language of demons gives a label, if not a shape, to the small and great instances of the mystery of evil. It matters not so much what language we use. Indeed the liturgy, its hymns and the scriptures use them all. It does, however, matter immensely that we take evil seriously, that we know it resides both inside and out, that we strive to recognize it, isolate it, and in the power of our baptism destroy it, and destroy it again and again, inside and out, whenever it reappears, as it continually will.

Romans 16:20   And we need not be afraid. As Paul wrote, in a nearly comical juxtaposition of words, "The God of peace will shortly crush *Psalm 110:1* Satan under your feet." Like Perpetua, we can climb up our ladders, making our enemy a footstool under our feet.

> Do you accept the idea of original sin?
> Compare images in paintings and sculptures of the serpent in Eden's tree.
> "The devil made me do it." Comment on this expression.
> What do we mean by exorcism, and when might exorcism be appropriate?

Make us so aware of your mercies,

O magnificent God,

that rejecting our demons is a joy.

Carry us

on your wings greater than any dragon's

into and out of the arena,

and raise us up at the last day.

IN THE NAME

ACTS 3:1 – 9

*Now Peter and John were going up to
the temple at the hour of prayer, the ninth
hour. And a man lame from birth was
being carried, whom they laid daily
at that gate of the temple which is called
Beautiful to ask alms of those who
entered the temple. Seeing Peter and
John about to go into the temple,
he asked for alms. And Peter directed his
gaze at him, with John, and said "Look at
us." And the man fixed his attention
upon them, expecting to receive something from them. But Peter said, "I have
no silver and gold, but I give you what I
have; in the name of Jesus Christ of
Nazareth, walk." And Peter took the
man by the right hand and raised him up;
and immediately his feet and ankles
were made strong. And leaping up he
stood and walked and entered the temple
with them, walking and leaping and
praising God. And all the people saw him
walking and praising God, and recognized the man as the one who sat for
alms at the Beautiful Gate of the temple,
and they were filled with wonder and
amazement at what had happened to him.*

> **"When Elijah had thrice poured out the barrels of water upon the cleft wood, he kindled at this prayer the fire from out of the water."**
>
> GREGORY OF NYSSA

The name of God

The story is told in the Acts of the Apostles that one day shortly after Pentecost, Peter and John, upon entering the temple, healed a lame man by evoking the "name of Jesus Christ of Nazareth." The spirit of the risen Christ had empowered them to change the world: Transforming the legs of a lame man was only the beginning. Annually, weekly, we come also to God's house to give thanks for the Spirit of the risen Christ, and at the doorstep we heal others, or heal ourselves, of one lameness or another. It is one way to think about baptism, whether on the night of the Vigil or daily in our lives: We place our lives under the power of the divine name.

There's a lot in the Bible about the power of God's name. It's as if God's "name" contains God's power and holiness. Hearing

the name of God, Moses is emboldened to face Pharaoh. Solomon *Exodus 3:14*
knows that God fills all heaven and earth, so he builds the temple *1 Kings 5:5*
to house at least the name of God. The name brings with it so
much divinity that Jews come to call God "The Name." The New
Testament makes the Christian claim that the name of God,
whether "the LORD" or "I AM" or even "my God," belongs also to *John 20:28*
Jesus. And though for the Jews the name became so taboo, so assid-
uously avoided because so radiantly holy, that it was never pro-
nounced, the Book of Revelation promises that at the end of time
all the faithful will wear the name on their foreheads. It will be *Revelation 3:12*
as if our baptismal sign shines forth, the lenten cross transformed
from ashes into light.

From the fourth century, life in the name

Gregory of Nyssa, a fourth-century bishop in present-day Turkey,
spent a lot of time contemplating the divine name. He and
two colleagues, Basil and another Gregory, are the triumvirate we
call "the Cappadocian Fathers," and it is their thinking about
the Trinity that birthed Christian trinitarian doctrine. In one of his
sermons which could well be entitled "Words around the Font,"
Gregory lays out numerous biblical reminders of baptism. Some we *Genesis 24:10–18*
are accustomed to: meeting Rebekah at the well, the crossing of *Exodus 14*
the Red Sea, the washing of Naaman the leper. But Gregory finds *2 Kings 5*
particular zest in retelling the story of Elijah and the prophets *1 Kings 18*
of Baal and Asherah.

 Recall that the king and queen of Israel had taken to invoking
the names of the Canaanite deities. Elijah decided to stage a
contest: Which name is most powerful: Baal, Asherah, or the
LORD? Elijah built an altar, the story says, "in the name of the LORD." *1 Kings 18:32*

And after pouring water three times over everything to souse the bull, the wood and the stones, he called on the name of Israel's god. As Gregory says, "He kindled at this prayer the fire from out of the water."

Gregory saw the scriptures with very different eyes than many of us. For Gregory, this ancient story is told to Christians not in order to enhance their knowledge of Canaanite religion, nor to judge the popularity of the goddess cult, nor to strain contemporary credulity, nor to disgust us (for Elijah and his buddies conclude the day by slaughtering the 450 Canaanite prophets). Rather, Christians use this narrative to help themselves imagine baptism. With powerful paradoxes, water brings forth fire. When water is poured out three times and the name of God is invoked, God's life is manifest.

The trinitarian name

Some Christians find the traditional name of the Trinity troubling. "Father, Son, Spirit" has been taught so meagerly and depicted so stupidly that to some people the name, far from opening up heaven to us all, seems decrepit and cramped. And of course, typical baptismal practice accentuates the three separate names by attaching one to each of the dousings of water, as if the water is about the three persons of the godhead. Gregory, along with other Eastern theologians, suggests instead that the three scoops of water or the three dips in the water are a sign of the three days of Christ in the grave, the water being for us the earth under which we must lie. The Cappadocians taught that the triune name is none other than the way to say God-in-Christ-for-us. That is, one way to say the name of Christ is to name out the Trinity. Even Augustine admitted that the Trinity cannot be adequately named and turned instead to the passage in Romans 11 which praises the triune God "from whom, through whom, and in whom all things exist."

Romans 11:36

So if not a male committee in the skies, what is the Trinity? Far from being the name of a dominant male who requires our submission, "Jesus" names a human being who lived and died, just as we live and die: not a stereotypicaly "masculine" human; not someone high up on a hierarchy of control, but one who gave puzzling answers and dined with the poor. Far from being yet another Zeus, the Trinity is a god already choosing loving interaction even before we enter the picture. Not a god in retirement, but God connected to the entire universe; not a god isolated in austere divinity, but God intertwined with humanity; not a god begrudging human life, but God permeating the community: This is some of what the name of the Trinity means.

Standing on this name

To stand on top of this name is to be supported in our connection with the universe and in our relationships with one another. It is to build upon all that is god-like in ourselves. As we call on the divine name, God calls us by our names, both the individual names by which we were baptized and the name of Christ, by which our community is known.

When I was in my twenties, I dropped my family name and replaced it with my husband's. Some years later, feeling the loss, I retrieved my name and hyphenated the two. Now I am back to my birth name. One hopes the baptismal journey is different. One's birth name is not discarded, but rather linked to the name of Christ, supported by the name of the Trinity. God's name does not erase our name, but instead underlies it. We are empowered, not displaced. And the name of God, let us hope, we do not outgrow.

What names for God have you been taught?

Can all divine names from other religions apply to our God? What do we mean by "our God"?

If you have ever changed your name, was it a positive experience?

If you were given a new name, what would be the absolute worst one to receive?

Your name is a bottomless sea,

O God,

connected, permeating,

supporting, overwhelming.

With your name,

O God, O Living One, give us life,

through Christ, the living one.

LIVING WATER

Jesus came to a city of Samaria, called Sychar, near the field that Jacob gave to his son Joseph. Jacob's well was there, and so Jesus, wearied from the journey, sat down beside the well. It was about the sixth hour.

There came a woman of Samaria to draw water. Jesus said to her, "Give me a drink." For his disciples had gone away into the city to buy food. The Samaritan woman said to Jesus, "How is it that you, a Jewish man, ask a drink of me, a woman of Samaria?" For Judeans have no dealings with Samaritans. Jesus answered the woman, "If you knew the gift of God, and who it is that is saying to you 'Give me a drink,' you would have asked him, and he would have given you living water." The woman said to him, "Sir, you have nothing to draw with, and the well is deep; where do you get the living water? Are you greater than our father Jacob, who gave us the well, and drank from it himself, and his children, and his cattle?" Jesus said to her, "Every one who drinks of this water will thirst again, but those who drink of the water that I shall give them will never thirst; the water that I shall give them will become in them a spring of water welling up to eternal life." The woman said to Jesus, "Sir, give me this water, that I may not thirst, nor come here to draw."

Jesus said to her, "Go, call your husband, and come here." The woman answered him, "I have no husband." Jesus said to her, "You are right in saying, 'I have no husband'; for you have had five husbands, and he whom you now have is not your husband; this you said truly." The woman said to Jesus, "Sir, I perceive that you are a prophet. Our forebears worshiped on this mountain; and you say that in Jerusalem is the place where it is proper to worship." Jesus said to her, "Woman, believe me, the hour is coming when neither on this mountain nor in Jerusalem will you worship the Father. You worship what you do not know; we worship what we know, for salvation is from the Jews. But the hour is coming, and now is, when the true worshipers will worship the Father in spirit and truth, for such worshipers the Father seeks. God is spirit, and those who worship God must worship in spirit and truth." The woman said to Jesus, "I know that Messiah is coming (the one who is called Christ); when that one comes, he will show us all things." Jesus said to her, "I who speak to you am the one."

Just then his disciples came. They marveled that Jesus was talking with a woman, but none said, "What do you wish?" or "Why are you talking with her?" So the woman left her water jar, and went away into the city, and said to the people, "Come, see someone who told me all that I ever did. Can this be the Christ?" They went out of the city and were coming to him.

Meanwhile the disciples besought Jesus, saying, "Rabbi, eat." But Jesus said to them, "I have food to eat of which you do not know." So the disciples said to one another, "Has any one brought him food?" Jesus said to them, "My food is to do the will and to accomplish the work of the one who sent me. Do you not say, 'There are yet four months, then comes the harvest?' I tell you, lift up your eyes, and see how the fields are already white for harvest. The reaper is already receiving wages, and gathers fruit for eternal life, so that the sower and reaper may rejoice together. For here the saying holds true, 'One sows and another reaps.' I sent you to reap that for which you did not labor; others have labored, and you have entered into their labor."

Many Samaritans from that city believed in Jesus because of the woman's testimony, "He told me all that I ever did." So when the Samaritans came to him, they asked him to stay with them; and Jesus stayed there two days. And many more believed because of his word. They said to the woman, "It is no longer because of your words that we believe, for we have heard for ourselves, and we know that this is indeed the Savior of the world."

> "The saints will be within their Creator
> just as the fish are in the sea; they
> will drink all they want, without
> becoming tired and without lessening
> the amount of water."
>
> MARGUERITE D'OINGT

Women out

When I was in high school visiting Yale University, the Art Gallery still had on display a reproduction of the third-century baptistry discovered at Dura-Europas. Its wall-painting of the woman at the well, and the fact that as a female I could not walk into the library's posh reading room, are all I recall of that visit to Yale. Both are gone now, the library's sign forbidding me entry as well as the facsimile of the woman at the well facing the font. The lectionary used during my childhood did not read John 4 at baptism or during Lent, and I smile to recall that even as a teenager I was drawn to an ancient baptistry and its biblical imagery.

The famous Samaritan woman whose name we do not know, although a good number of men of her time knew much more about her than her name, shared the daily task still shared by many poor women today. Twice a day women walk the distance to the local well and carry back on their head or shoulders the pots of water needed for living. This back-breaking task has long and far been assigned to women, as if women know better than men that people must drink, cook, wash vessels, wash clothes, wash themselves, bathe wounds, clean the house, water the animals. The barley mash must be boiled up each day. Whether washing off the newborn, washing off the corpse, washing out her monthly rags, or wiping up the family vomit, it is the woman in many societies who aches for a source of endlessly flowing water, a fountain of pure water filling every need before it arises. Not these two heavy waterpots full, not a cistern with its sediment, not even a well which might run dry: We want a river of clean water, a lake, a sea, near the house, but safe within its banks, ready for our use.

Finding baptism

John's gospel says the Samaritan woman was shown the fountain. She was invited to take all the water she needed. The early centuries of the church, and now we again, have seen in the Samaritan woman an image of us all. We all search in the wrong place for refreshment, lugging home water which gives out or goes bad; we continuously need more water; we are always somewhat thirsty, dirty or raw. We thought to find water there, down at the stream, and were surprised to find it here, directly before us. Turning around —the word is conversion—we find a water source we had not even imagined. Baptism, says the church, is this water source, this fountain of God, this conversation with Christ, this gift of self-knowledge, this sense of mission, this true religious rite, this conversion of life.

Still thirsty

Sometimes we talk as if, by providing us with the everlasting fountain, baptism eradicates our thirst. Perhaps you too have read the sentence, "These rites should complete the conversion of the elect." But we know that to be wishful thinking. The Samaritan woman, *Genesis 29:1–12* whose life was so turned around, had to come back the next day to Jacob's well for water, and when the two days were up and Jesus left town, her thirst for God returned. We are like her: The water is ours, yet we still know our endless need. "Continuing conversion" is one way the church has articulated this. Each year we need to find Jesus again. Each year we are surprised by being shown the fountain.

Medieval monastic women knew well this continuing need. From the eleventh through the fourteenth centuries, dozens of women, perhaps frustrated by a church and world that pushed women away from much that might sustain them, found by interior vision the divine fountain they sought. One such mystic was Marguerite d'Oingt, a thirteenth-century upper-class prioress of a Carthusian monastery. Within that rigorous lifestyle of utter renunciation, Marguerite had such lush visions that, nearly sick with the surfeit of images, she wrote them down, in Latin, French and Provençal, to release herself from their power. In her *Mirror* is a passage about this continuing conversion: "The saints will be within their Creator just as the fish are in the sea; they will drink all they want, without becoming tired and without lessening the amount of water." Even a hermit needs to drink daily, but Marguerite testified that the saints live in God, who is their perpetual sea of flowing water. Living water is always theirs, surrounding them, flowing through them, buoying up their entire life.

Women in

Before baptism and each Lent thereafter we sit beside these women. The first found living water for the first time, the second swam in it her whole life. The Samaritan was a woman of the world, the Carthusian a celibate recluse: Both needed the living water that God alone pours out. And for us who are thirsty, here is the good news: No sign excludes us.

Before baptism and each Lent thereafter we receive the creed. Perhaps it has come for the first time, or perhaps we recite it weekly year in and year out. In either case, along with the Samaritan who received a new way to worship God and to know herself, and along with the Carthusian who received such visions of life with God that 700 years later her words dance off the page, we receive words for our worship. The creed calls us back to the font where the Samaritan sits; it stands us inside the ecstasy in which the Carthusian writes. We take in the living water, as the water has taken us in, for here is the good news: The creed includes us. Like the sea, matrix to zillions of pieces of life, the liturgy washes us together to Christ. Like the sea, Christ bears us to God. Like the sea, God sustains us with living water. Here is enough life for us all.

Do women know more about human need than men do?

Why does the story of the Samaritan woman include allusions to her sexual past?

What is gained by a life of self-denial? What is lost?

Have you ever nearly drowned?

Fill us inside,

surround us outside,

spring up beside us,

flow alongside us,

O God,

living water, boundless sea,

eternal fountain, flowing river,

quenching thirst we knew we had,

meeting needs before and beyond our knowing.

OUR SIGHT RESTORED

JOHN 9 : 1 – 41

Passing by, Jesus saw someone who was blind from birth. And Jesus's disciples asked him, "Rabbi, who sinned, this person or his parents, that he was born blind?" Jesus answered, "It was not that this person sinned, or his parents, but that the works of God might be made manifest in him. We must work the works of the one who sent me, while it is day; night comes, when no one can work. As long as I am in the world, I am the light of the world." Saying this, Jesus spat on the ground and made clay of the spittle and anointed the man's eyes with the clay, saying to him, "Go, wash in the pool of Siloam" (which means Sent). So he went and washed and came back seeing. The neighbors and those who had seen him before as a beggar, said, "Is not this the person who used to sit and beg?" Some said, "It is he"; others said, "No, but he is like him." He said, "I am the one." They said to him, "Then how were your eyes opened?" He answered, "The man called Jesus made clay and anointed my eyes and said to me, 'Go to Siloam and wash'; so I went and washed and received my sight." They said to him, "Where is he?" He said, "I do not know." They brought to the Pharisees the one who had formerly been blind. Now it was a sabbath day when Jesus made the clay and opened his eyes. The Pharisees again asked him how he had received his sight.

And he said to them, "He put clay on my eyes, and I washed, and I see." Some of the Pharisees said, "This man is not from God, for he does not keep the sabbath." But others said, "How can a sinner do such signs?" There was a division among them. So they again said to the blind man, "What do you say about him, since he has opened your eyes?" He said, "He is a prophet."

The Jewish people did not believe that he had been blind and had received his sight, until they had called the parents of the one who had received his sight, and asked them, "Is this your son, who you say was born blind? How then does he now see?" His parents answered, "We know that this is our son, and that he was born blind; but how he now sees we do not know, nor do we know who opened his eyes. Ask him; he is of age, he will speak for himself." His parents said this because they feared the Jewish people who had already agreed that any one confessing him to be Christ was to be put out of the synagogue. Therefore his parents said, "He is of age, ask him."

So for the second time they called the one who had been blind, and said to him, "Give God the praise; we know that this man is a sinner." He answered, "Whether he is a sinner, I do not know; one thing I know, that though I was blind, now I see." They said to him, "What did he do to you? How did he open your eyes?" He answered them, "I have told you already, and you would not listen. Why do you want to hear it again? Do you too want to become his disciples?" And they reviled him, saying "You are his disciple, but we are disciples of Moses. We know that God has spoken to Moses, but as for this person, we do not know where he comes from." The man answered, "Why, this is a marvel! You do not know where he comes from, and yet he opened my eyes. We know that God does not listen to sinners, but God listens to any one who is devout and does God's will. Never since the world began has it been heard that any one opened the eyes of one born blind. If this person were not from God, he could do nothing." They answered him, "You were born in utter sin, and would you teach us?" And they cast him out.

Jesus heard that they had cast him out, and having found him, Jesus said, "Do you believe in the Man of Heaven?" He answered, "And who is the Man of Heaven, sir, that I may believe in him?" Jesus said to him, "You have seen him: the one speaking to you is the one." He said, "Lord, I believe"; and he worshiped Jesus. Jesus said, "For judgment I came into this world, that those who do not see may see, and that those who see may become blind." Some of the Pharisees near Jesus heard this, and they said to him, "Are we also blind?" Jesus said to them, "If you were blind, you would have no guilt, but now that you say, 'We see,' your guilt remains."

> "You went, you washed, you came to the altar, you began to see what you had not seen before."

A M B R O S E

A *darkness not my fault*

One way to talk about human distress is to use the metaphor of darkness. No matter how acute or how dull our sight, we can say that the earth is a dark place. There is the darkness of the human heart, with its hidden corners of evil, its walls of fear, its many enigmas like corridors never exposed to daylight. But there is also the darkness of the outside world: my personal contributions to evil fit right into a planet blighted by systems of evil. One race murders another, a nation dominates whomever it can, the moneyed bully the poor, each ethnic group has its own memories of horror inflicted and horror received, each sex manipulates the other, and the very technology that brings light to my nights inevitably results in darkness for someone, somewhere. We can never get ahead of, or even catch up to, the problems that require our correction. So you're sitting around with nothing to do? How about contacting a legislator about an international crisis? How about volunteering for a blood drive? How about tutoring a poor kid downtown?

That I live with some prerogatives in this world means that willy-nilly I contribute to this darkness. Whether or not I realize it, I am in fact blowing out candles here and there. But there is a second truth: I am caught in social evils not of my own making. I was born into patterns of injustice and destruction that are not my fault. How I deal with that darkness is, yes, my responsibility. But that the situation is this terrible is the well that I was dropped into at birth and within which I am flailing about.

Christ our light

The story in John 9 of the man born blind can speak to this aspect of the human condition. That the man exists in total darkness is not his fault. Nor is it his parents' fault. The blind man is not ignorant of the darkness—and let us beware lest "blindness" get misused as a metaphor: "I was too blind to realize that my kid was on drugs." Quite the contrary. The blind live in perpetual, throbbing realization of the darkness they inhabit. And like a blind person who knows the edges in the darkness far more clearly than a sighted person does, we may with our daily news services and endless editorials and tomes of analysis know the measurements and characteristics of our darkness with perfect accuracy. But having the data does not eliminate, or even much illuminate, the darkness.

The Christian faithful believe that Christ is the light. Enacted annually at the great Easter Vigil, recalled in the gospel for Christmas Day, remembered each night at evening prayer, recognized in the candle at the casket, and ritualized by the candle at baptism, "Christ our light" is our claim. It is not that Christ does away with darkness, that the baptized walk about in perpetual light. No, speech about perpetual light shining upon us is the hope of the resurrection, the promise of God's light finally victorious over death's night. But not now. Now the paschal candle is a reminder of what often seems a small flicker in the darkness that continues to envelop us all.

Knowing the darkness

So if the world remains dark, what does the illumination of baptism actually do? Ambrose, the fourth century bishop of Milan, said it this way: "You went, you washed, you came to the altar, you began to see what you had not seen before." You began to see the light of Christ, yes. But you also began to see more clearly the world's darkness. Think of Ambrose, informed of the emperor Theodosius's cruelty in a heartless slaughter of 7000 townspeople. Seeing into this darkness, Ambrose barred the emperor from communing until he publicly repented. Think again of Ambrose, recognizing the heresies that the empress Justina supported. Seeing into this darkness, Ambrose blocked the empress's plan to take over some of Milan's churches. The light of his baptism did not take Ambrose out of the darkness but gave him a beacon with which to recognize the dread shapes it obscured.

Ambrose stands before us a sign of baptismal illumination. Baptized on November 24, 373, he was consecrated bishop one week later: hardly a goal to which any sensible Christian would aspire, but an extraordinary example of one off whom the light of Christ reflected. People saw the world more clearly because of him. In 387 Ambrose baptized Augustine, and we still can read his homilies to the catechumens about the entire baptismal process. He composed lucid Latin hymns for all the assembly, not just the choir, and we ought not be surprised that his most renowned hymns, one for morning, one for evening, and one for Advent, all employ light imagery.

Beginning to see

Acts 9:1–9 Perhaps for some Christians the illumination of baptism is like the blinding flash from heaven knocking Saul off his high horse, making everything either brilliantly light or utterly dark. But for many Christians, Ambrose speaks a closer truth: We begin to see. Some Christians begin this seeing as infants: I was seven weeks old at my illumination. Others begin to see as adults, and some, like the Roman emperor Constantine, on their deathbeds. But we all come weekly to celebrate the light, to absorb more of it into our faces, to see one another shining. The blind leading the blind, we help one another grope toward the light that is God. Perhaps we finally come to recognize even God in the center of the darkness itself.

Why is darkness a very limited way to talk about evil and distress? What is good and what is beautiful about darkness?

Read the front page of today's newspaper and try to determine who is at fault in each conflict. Where do we stop?

What is the responsibility of each contemporary citizen to the native peoples of the land?

Who are the Ambrose-like people alive today?

Our room has no lights;

our legs are gashed by sharp edges,

our feet stumble over the piles of trash.

We see and cannot see in this darkness.

O God, illumine our chaos:

Be in our darkness,

and let there be light.

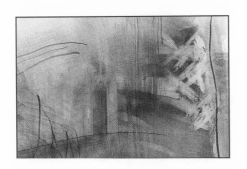

OUR GRAVES OPENED

JOHN 11:1 – 53

Now a certain man was ill, Lazarus of Bethany, the village of Mary and her sister Martha. It was Mary who anointed the Lord with ointment and wiped his feet with her hair, whose brother Lazarus was ill. So the sisters sent to Jesus, saying, "Lord, he whom you love is ill." But when Jesus heard it he said, "This illness is not unto death; it is for the glory of God, so that the Son of God may be glorified by means of it."

Now Jesus loved Martha and her sister and Lazarus. So when Jesus heard that Lazarus was ill, he stayed two days longer in the place where he was. Then after this he said to the disciples, "Let us go into Judea again." The disciples said to him, "Rabbi, the Judeans were but now seeking to stone you, and are you going there again?" Jesus answered, "Are there not twelve hours in the day? Those who walk in the day do not stumble because they see the light of this world. But those who walk in the night do stumble, because the light is not in them." Thus Jesus spoke, and then said to them, "Our friend Lazarus has fallen asleep, but I go to awake him out of sleep." The disciples said to him, "Lord, if he has fallen asleep, he will recover." Now Jesus had spoken of his death, but they thought that he meant taking rest in sleep. Then Jesus told them plainly, "Lazarus is dead; and for your sake I am glad that I was not there, so

that you may believe. But let us go to him." Thomas, called the Twin, said to the other disciples, "Let us also go, that we may die with him."

Now when Jesus came, he found that Lazarus had already been in the tomb four days. Bethany was near Jerusalem, about two miles off, and many of the Judeans had come to Martha and Mary to console them concerning their brother. When Martha heard that Jesus was coming, she went and met him, while Mary sat in the house. Martha said to Jesus, "Lord, if you had been here, my brother would not have died. And even now I know that whatever you ask from God, God will give you." Jesus said to her, "Your brother will rise again." Martha said to Jesus, "I know that he will rise again in the resurrection of the last day." Jesus said to her, "I am the resurrection and the life; they who believe in me, though they die, yet shall they live, and whoever lives and believes in me shall never die. Do you believe this?" She said to him, "Yes, Lord; I believe that you are the Christ, the Son of God, the one who is coming into the world."

Having said this, Martha went and called her sister Mary, saying quietly, "The Teacher is here and is calling for you." And when Mary heard it, she rose quickly and went to him. Now Jesus had not yet come to the village, but was still in the place where Martha had met him. When the Jewish people who were with her in the house, consoling her, saw Mary rise quickly and go out, they followed her, supposing that she was going to the tomb to weep there. Then Mary, when she came where Jesus was and saw him, fell at his feet, saying to him, "Lord, if you had been here, my brother would not have died." When Jesus saw her weeping, and the Jewish people who came with her also weeping, he was deeply moved in spirit and troubled; and Jesus said, "Where have you laid him?" They said to him, "Lord, come and see." Jesus wept. So the Jewish people said, "See how he loved him!" But some of them said, "Could not the one who opened the eyes of the blind man have kept this man from dying?"

Then Jesus, deeply moved again, came to the tomb; it was a cave, and a stone lay upon it. Jesus said, "Take away the stone." Martha, the sister of the deceased, said to Jesus, "Lord, by this time there will be an odor, for he has been dead for four days." Jesus said to her, "Did I not tell you that if you would believe you would see the glory of God?" So they took away the stone. And Jesus lifted up his eyes and said, "Father, I thank you that you have heard me. I knew that you hear me always, but

I have said this on account of the people standing by, that they may believe that you sent me." Having said this, Jesus cried with a loud voice, "Lazarus, come out." The dead man came out, his hands and feet bound with bandages, and his face wrapped with a cloth. Jesus said to them, "Unbind him, and let him go."

Many of the Judeans therefore, who had come with Mary and had seen what Jesus did, believed in him; but some of them went to the Pharisees and told them what Jesus had done. So the chief priests and the Pharisees gathered the council, and said, "What are we to do? For this person performs many signs. If we let him go on thus, every one will believe in him, and the Romans will come and destroy both our holy place and our nation." But one of them, Caiaphas, who was high priest that year, said to them, "You know nothing at all; you do not understand that it is expedient for you that one person should die for the people, and that the whole nation should not perish." He did not say this of his own accord, but being high priest that year he prophesied that Jesus should die for the nation, and not for the nation only, but to gather into one the children of God who are scattered abroad. So from that day on they took counsel how to put Jesus to death.

> "Let us receive this teaching, that they who are alive may live, and they who are dead may return to life."

A U G U S T I N E

How to do research on this one?

To write the section about John 9 without saying flagrantly ignorant things about blind people, I listened to Donna and her guide dog Curly Connor tell me what the blind life is like. We are now at John's Lazarus story, but we have no one dead for four days to report to us what it was like. We are in fact like the brothers of the rich man in Luke's parable of another Lazarus, a beggar: No one will rise *Luke 16:19-31* from the dead to tell us of our future. And what about those people who have been clinically dead and live again to speak of light and peace? Did they arrive at heaven's gate, or is their sensation a consequence of the endorphin surge that physicians note often accompanies the body's final release?

The story in John 11 of the raising of Lazarus is matter-of-fact and graphic: The corpse stinks. The story is also beyond our grasp, beyond our experience: Lazarus who was dead has returned to life. Connecting biblical stories to our lives is never "elementary, my dear Watson," but this story is more problematic than most.

Being dead

Although we haven't been dead yet, we have all been bound up by winding sheets. Something functions as our shroud, something wraps our jaw up or ties our arms motionless. There are those days, perhaps those years, when those around us must call us back from the dead. Hey you, out of that coffin! It's not time yet! You look absolutely awful in white! Raise that lid! You're not alone, you know. Our family and friends gather around with shovels to exhume us, to slap us around a bit to get the blood flowing again.

Different people, different fatalities. Sometimes we have let too much of the world's death in, and like cancer, it takes over. Sometimes the death of another person has been so contagious that we are dying of that same death. Sometimes we've hidden in such an airtight room, just me in here, that death comes by the asphyxiation of isolation. Who knows all the reasons that we choose not to get dressed in the morning but lie around in a shroud instead? Who knows what starts us off stinking?

So what's the meaning of the story?

Some Christians believe with Augustine that Lazarus's resuscitation literally occurred, historically, albeit miraculously. Others suggest that the story is the evangelist's supreme illustration, the gospel's *John 1:1–18* seventh sign, of the theme of the prologue in John 1, that Christ is God's life for the world. All agree that what the story narrates is not a resurrection, not that ultimate transformation of the body and nature into a new creation beyond this life and death. Rather, this gift of a second life to Jesus' dead friend is used by the gospel writer as a sign that the resurrection is Christ. Even Augustine, who accepted the story as fact, in preaching about the three gospel narratives in which the dead are raised to life, taught that the Lazarus story describes not resuscitated corpses but those of us buried by sinful habits who are called to stand before Christ. Not Lazarus's adventure, but Christ is the resurrection and the life.

As an image of new life in Christ, Lazarus is about Christian baptism. The mighty event of our baptism is like the call of Christ disturbing the silence of our tomb, and the renewal of baptism is the continuous unbinding of our grave clothes, the daily unwrapping of that winding sheet that is forever obstructing our walk toward the dominion of God.

Receiving this teaching

This story in the gospel of John offers us two articles of faith. Not my own strength, not a doctor's skill, not a generally positive attitude that people with my personality can successfully cultivate: These are not my resurrection and my life. Christ is. God is life, and our life comes in baptismal relationship to divine life. The story is about receiving life from God, not about avoiding the cemetery.

But the gospel urges a second truth upon us. Receiving the divine life gives another dimension to our human life. Usually we speak as if that dimension follows our life in time and exceeds it vastly in happiness. And so we imagine heaven, where life is eternal and joy supreme. Perhaps such a heaven is true: we have no Lazarus to ask. But perhaps that second dimension—"Whoever lives in me will never die"—is a baptized life, realized now and here, simultaneous to our lifetime, and exceeding normal everyday existence not in happiness but in "truth."

John 18:38 Yes, Pilate, a good question: What is truth?

According to the gospel of John, the raising of Lazarus is the direct cause of Jesus' arrest and execution. Lazarus receives life, but Jesus must give it up. It is odd, it is incongruous, that popular Christianity assumes that the sign of divine life is joy, as if following Christ is the same thing as following your bliss. You'd think we'd have learned by now. The purpose of Lazarus's death, said Jesus, was to glorify God, but biblical exegetes remind us that for John, God's glory is released when Christ is lifted up on the cross. John John 10:10 means something by "the abundant life" that we baptized folk have not yet understood.

Receiving the teaching together

The name Lazarus means "God helps." He lived in Bethany, which means "house of affliction." It ought not surprise us, neophytes and old-timers alike, that God helps us in our house of affliction by sending the community to help us. Even when we try to respond to the words of Christ, we cannot unbind ourselves. It is the Marys and the Marthas who unbind us. So the weekly liturgy affords us occasion to unbind each other, for Christ uses his body to call forth and nurture divine life. Christ is our resurrection and life by means of the assembled believers, whether distributing bread and wine or digging up the graves of all of us so often prematurely buried alive. Perhaps this is why Augustine, in preaching about this text, used the plural: "They who are alive, they who are dead." "The body of Christ for you" is, after all, a plural "you." Myself unbound, my arms are free to unbind the person sitting behind me in church.

What's your experience with dead bodies?

Do you assume you will be embalmed? What do you think about this process?

What stories can you tell of unbinding?

What about you stinks the most? Why?

Come this time on time, O God,

to our house of affliction,

and help us.

Give us life,

the stone rolled away,

the grave clothes laid aside,

the community assembled,

that we may live abundantly

whatever you mean by truth.

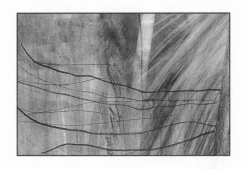

OUR FEET WASHED

JOHN 13:1 – 20

Now before the feast of Passover, when Jesus knew that his hour had come to depart out of this world to the Father, having loved his own who were in the world, he loved them to the end. And during supper, when the devil had already put it into the heart of Judas Iscariot, Simon's son, to betray him, Jesus, knowing that the Father had given all things into his hands, and that he had come from God and was going to God, rose from supper, laid aside his garments, and girded himself with a towel. Then he poured water into a basin, and began to wash the disciples' feet, and to wipe them with the towel with which he was girded. Jesus came to Simon Peter; and Peter said to him, "Lord, do you wash my feet?" Jesus answered him, "What I am doing you do not know now, but afterward you will understand." Peter said to him, "You shall never wash my feet." Jesus answered Peter, "If I do not wash you, you have no part in me." Simon Peter said to Jesus, "Lord, not my feet only but also my hands and my head!" Jesus said to him, "Those who have bathed do not need to wash, except for their feet, but they are clean all over; and you are clean, but not every one of you." For Jesus knew who was to betray him; that was why he said, "You are not all clean."

When Jesus had washed their feet, and taken his garments, and resumed his place, he said to them, "Do you know what I have done to you? You call me Teacher and Lord; and you are right, for so I am. If I then, your Lord and Teacher, have washed your feet, you also ought wash one another's feet. For I have given you an example, that you should do as I have done to you. Truly, truly, I say to you, slaves are not greater than their masters; nor those who are sent greater than the one who sent them. If you know these things, blessed are you if you do them."

> "He who gathers together the waters of the sea as in a vessel now pours water into a basin."

CYRIL OF ALEXANDRIA

The church and the footwashing

At the start of the Triduum, as the catechumens and the baptized head toward the Vigil, we hear the narrative in John 13 of Jesus washing the disciples' feet. Over time, the footwashing ritual acquired various meanings and uses in the church. Benedictine monks used the footwashing as a sign of hospitality to guests. Seventh Day Adventists connect it so closely to communion that they do both rites on the same Sunday, four times a year, men in one circle, women in another, everyone washing a partner's feet, then joining together for the bread and wine. For some of the ordained, the footwashing is about clerical identity, for they claim that the ritual can be performed only by clergy. Many Christians have taught that the *mandatum*, the command, is not to the footwashing itself but to loving one another, and out of nervousness or laziness or stunted imaginations have omitted the ritual altogether.

Whatever else the ritual has been or might be, we are here considering words around the font, and the words about the footwashing stand before us. Here are words about the pouring of water, the sharing with one another in Christ, our loving the community as the body of Christ. For those of us reviving the ritual, the water pouring over our feet from the pitcher into the basin is a reminder of baptism, God's grace flowing over our entire life. I kneel before you to wash your feet: a reminder of baptism, which re-created me as a person ready at all times to serve you. You kneel before me to wash my feet: a reminder of baptism, which reshapes me as part of your life, indeed, as part of your very body, to care for. For what is common to both the sacrament of baptism and the symbol of footwashing is water poured out as a sign of grace, I serving you, you caring for me.

The church and Christ

The footwashing points us not only toward baptism, but also toward Christ. Jesus concluded his ritual by instructing the disciples that all these things were taking place—the meal, the washing, the betrayal, his death—so that we may believe that "I AM." Many Bible translations cast this as "I am he." But check the footnotes to John 13:19, and see that here is one of John's passages in which *John 13:19* Christ takes on the very name of God. "I AM," God calls out from the burning bush to Moses. "I AM" is the name of God hidden *Ex 3:14* in the promises of Second Isaiah. "I AM," Jesus calls out to the *Is 48:12* challenging crowd, and John 8 records that "they picked up stones to throw at him." This man, this goad, this enigma, this guy here *Jn 8:58* is the great I AM?

The footwashing leads us to God through Christ, whom we can call by the mysterious divine name. The footwashing leads us to God in Christ, because we kneel before that body of Christ when kneeling before one another, towel in hand. I AM ignited a bush without destroying it; I AM, the Eternal One, volunteers for kitchen duty.

Tumultuous waters

Jesus filled a basin with water. Cyril, the fifth-century bishop of Alexandria, saw in this text a reference to the poems of the Hebrew Bible in which God's creative work at the beginning of time included damming up the chaotic seas, setting up boundaries to contain the raging waters. As the poem of Job has it, God yells out to the primordial, proud waves, "Thus far shall you come, and

Job 38:11 no farther!" God constrains the sea so that the world may be created. Christ fills a basin with water so that the church may be created. A fellow worshiper pours water over my feet into a large bowl so that I, a new I, will be created.

Years ago a student suggested replacing the footwashing with a ritualized shoe-shining. It was a clever idea, but superficial, shallower than the water in Thursday's basin. For the footwashing is far more than a sign of servitude. To all who watch it and to all who perform it, it is a call to I AM, a call to God's new life. Like nascent life emerging from the waters at the origins of earth's time, our new life springs from the seas contained by God's mighty word. The ritual is not literally about washing already-clean feet. It is rather about encountering divine creation.

The church and each other

In many religions, to serve the deity one lays food before an image of the appropriate goddess or god. In contrast, Christianity invites the baptized to serve God by offering food to the poor. We do not serve God by pouring water over a statue. Instead, we serve one another by daily care and loving attention.

Perhaps our rituals are in some ways more difficult. It seems to me that a bejeweled divine image could be far easier to honor than our families, our parish, our neighbors, our fellow citizens. Everyone know that a magnificent depiction of divinity, a prize-winning religious painting or a gilded shrine is far more attractive than a dying great-aunt, and many of us are far more likely to have "a religious experience" standing in Paris's magnificent Sainte-Chapelle or before Marc Chagall's biblical stained glass windows than when changing a baby. So it is that Martin Luther enjoins Christian fathers to change their infants' diapers as one of the ways they are to serve their God.

I have to admit that I'd rather don my alb and do profound bows than remove the robe and on hands and knees clean up the world's messes. Baptism, however, makes both activities one. The incarnation means that everything that seems sacred, teeming with divine power, takes its deepest meaning from the ordinary. Creation is tied to footwashing. The world's religions are filled with the devout kneeling before a creator, but a deity who kneels before the people to serve them, that's a different story. It's an intriguing religion into which we are baptized.

Read and discuss the I AM passages in the gospel of John.

How is the footwashing not like baptism?

Our culture devalues service to others or seeks to elevate it with decent pay. Is the Christian emphasis on service to others reactionary?

How and when is God in our neighbor? How and when is God not in our neighbor?

O God, be our God,

containing the seas,

pouring water into a basin,

washing us yet again.

Make us into us,

your body in the world,

our feet washed,

ready to serve.

A NEW BIRTH

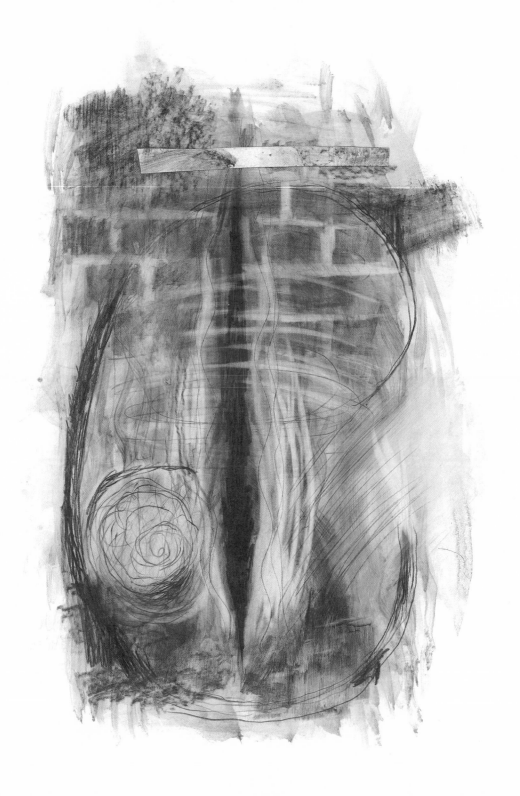

JOHN 3:1 – 21

Now there was one of the pharisees, named Nicodemus, a ruler of the Jewish people. He came to Jesus by night and said to him, "Rabbi, we know that you are a teacher come from God; for no one can do these signs that you do, except with the presence of God." Jesus said to Nicodemus, "Truly, truly, I say to you, unless one is born anew, one cannot see the dominion of God." Nicodemus said to Jesus, "How can a person be born when that person is old? Can one enter a second time into the womb and be born?" Jesus answered, "Truly, truly, I say to you, unless one is born of water and the Spirit, one cannot enter the dominion of God. That which is born of the flesh is flesh, and that which is born of the Spirit is spirit. Do not marvel that I said to you, 'You must be born anew.' The wind blows where it wills, and you hear the sound of it, but you do not know whence it comes or whither it goes; so it is with every one who is born of the Spirit." Nicodemus said to Jesus, "How can this be?" Jesus answered him, "Are you a teacher of Israel, and yet you do not understand this? Truly, truly, I say to you, we speak of what we know, and bear witness to what we have seen; but you do not receive our testimony. If I have told you earthly things and you do not believe, how can you believe if I tell you heavenly things? No one has ascended into heaven but the one who descended from heaven, the Man of Heaven. And as Moses lifted up the serpent in the wilderness, so must the Man of Heaven be lifted up, that whoever believes in that one may have eternal life."

For God loved the world in this way, that God gave the Son, the only begotten one, that whoever believes in him should not perish but have eternal life. For God sent the Son into the world, not to condemn the world, but that through the Son the world might be saved. Those who believe in him are not condemned; those who do not believe are condemned already, because they have not believed in the name of the only Son of God. And this is the judgment, that the light has come into the world, and people loved darkness rather than light, because their deeds were evil. For those who do evil hate the light, and do not come to the light, lest their deeds should be exposed. But they who do what is true come to the light, that it may be clearly seen that their deeds have been wrought in God.

> "Run, then, forward to the mother who experiences no pains of labor although she cannot count the number of those to whom she gives birth."

ZENO

Being born

The gospel of John introduces us to Nicodemus, a devout Jew who loved God's Torah and continuously sought for more of the presence of God. At night, when most human births occur, he found Jesus. Nicodemus wished to inquire whether the miracle worker had an inside track on the road toward God. But the Jesus of John's gospel, like the Jesus of Mark's, doesn't give straight answers. Rather, we hear enigmatic comments about our being born from above, of water and Spirit. Instead of clear directions, Jesus offers a process in a metaphor: new birth.

Although some people claim to recall their own birth, I do not. What I do recall is the birth of each of my daughters, and the experience of at least this one woman dismisses as twaddle much of the poetic talk about the glories of childbirth. A recent television commercial for cameras showed a hospital delivery room in which the mother, one minute after cheerfully pushing out her baby, reaches up to help the confused father load the family camera correctly. That isn't how it was with me. With me, as with countless women, nearly every step of the process went wrong, Mother Nature capable of yielding up death quite as freely as life. There is a theory that human labor is so painful because our skulls have grown too big for the birth canal, the very thing that makes us human promising agony at the start.

God bearing us

The myths of many religions contain stories of the deity bearing the world or its human species. In the Hebrew tradition only traces of these stories remain. The sometimes ill-translated poem in Deuteronomy 32 chides the people of Israel for forgetting their mother God. Poems in Isaiah compare God to a mother in labor and a mother nursing. It may be that the word "mercy," one of God's primary characteristics, derives from an ancient word for womb. Yet always in the Hebrew tradition, it is neither the earth nor the individual but the whole people who is born of God. Nature has been turned toward salvation.

Deuteronomy 32:18

Isaiah 66:9–12

But more distinctive is that the Jewish and Christian traditions have shied away from talk of God's bearing us. The metaphor of birth from God too readily suggests that we are made of the same stuff as God, an alluring idea that monotheists must continually refute. One biblical passage that talks outright of our being born of God, 1 John, is marked by the danger inherent in the metaphor. The author uses the metaphor to maintain that those truly born of God have no sin, a logical inference from the image, but demonstrably untrue.

1 John 3:9

A buffer on the delivery table

The New Testament usually introduces an intermediary into the birth metaphor. Something else is in the sentence along with God the mother and us the infant. John 3 says that we are born from above, of water and the Spirit; 1 Peter says that we are born through the word, by divine mercy; the allegory in Galatians 4 adds "according to the Spirit." Like the Hebrew cicumlocutions that refer to "the Name" or "the Shekinah" rather than to God's very being, these phrases put just that little bit of distance between the Creator and the creatures.

1 Peter 1:23

Galatians 4:29

The Christian poetic tradition has usually imagined the church as the medium of our birth. Patristic preachers could revel in the metaphor of birth without implying that we too closely resembled the being of God. One of many examples comes from the fourth century, when Zeno, an African who became bishop in Verona, wrote in near ecstasy of our baptism into Mother Church: "Run, then, forward to the mother who experiences no pains of labor although she cannot count the number of those to whom she gives birth." At least in this passage the mother is spared labor pains in her bearing of us all.

Ah, but play with any metaphor too long and like a cat it leaps around to scratch you. With the church as mother, God becomes our father, and we are again on that symbolic road with ruts so deep that the muffler of our car is scraping on the ground and our tires can hardly reach the pavement any more.

Constructing the metaphor

With all the danger signs in place, let us play with the metaphor in John 3. It's not, after all, as if we are naturally born of God, as if we are little godlets worshiping ourselves as the ultimate focus of our life. Rather, baptism introduces an anomoly: Human beings receive again the likeness of God; we don the mystery of generation from the divine. Although we are not gods, we are remade as something of God. There is some mirror, some memory, some resemblance. Like Jesus' twin, we live somehow like God, resembling the Trinity in our endless care for each other.

The birth was not easy, but God was up to it, pushing us out to live on our own and then enfolding us whenever we, quite unable to live alone, would cry out for warmth and milk. God the mother, ready to feed, ready to correct, some nurturing here, some disciplining there, bears us all, feeds us all, carries us all, rears us all, sends us off and welcomes us home, there at our beginning in baptism, there at our end at burial.

Confounding the metaphor

There's something very clever about how Zeno uses the image of baptism as childbirth. In Zeno's invitations to baptism, the mother is the church, though one could read these passages so that the mother is God herself. In either case we are to run toward our birthing. Run, as an adult can, toward our own childbirth? I have heard it said that baptism treats infants like adults, by asking them for a life commitment, and treats adults like infants, by calling them newborn. So Zeno confounds the metaphor: We are both infants receiving new birth and adults seeing our destiny, for baptism is both like new birth and not like new birth. As with all our images for baptism, the language works, and doesn't.

What's your favorite birth story? What's your least favorite?

How is the image of God as mother helpful for you? How is the image problematic?

Those of you who have never given or could never give birth: How do you respond to the image of baptism as birthing?

Do we really run toward God? Does God really run toward us?

Your womb waters,

O mother God,

gave life to us all.

Now wash off our bodies

the blood of your Son,

and nurse us, we beg you,

when we wail.

ANOINTED WITH THE SPIRIT

ROMANS 8:1 – 39

There is therefore now no condemnation for those who are in Christ Jesus. For the law of the Spirit of life in Christ Jesus has set me free from the law of sin and death. For God has done what the law, weakened by the flesh, could not do: sending God's own Son in the likeness of sinful flesh and for sin, God condemned sin in the flesh, in order that the just requirement of the law might be fulfilled in us, who walk not according to the flesh but according to the Spirit. For those who live according to the flesh set their minds on the things of the flesh, but those who live according to the Spirit set their minds on the things of the Spirit. To set the mind on the flesh is death, but to set the mind on the Spirit is life and peace. For the mind that is set on the flesh is hostile to God; it does not submit to God's law, indeed it cannot; and those who are in the flesh cannot please God.

But you are not in the flesh, you are in the spirit, if in fact the Spirit of God dwells in you. Any one who does not have the Spirit of Christ does not belong to Christ. But if Christ is in you, although your bodies are dead because of sin, your spirits are alive because of righteousness. If the Spirit of the one who raised Jesus from the dead dwells in you, the one who raised Christ Jesus from the dead will give life to your mortal bodies also through this Spirit dwelling in you.

So then, my dear people, we are debtors, not to the flesh, to live according to the flesh—for if you live according to the flesh you will die, but if by the Spirit you put to death the deeds of the body you will live. For all who are led by the Spirit of God are children of God. For you did not receive the spirit of slavery to fall back into fear, but you have received the spirit of adoption. When we cry, "Abba! Father!" it is that very Spirit bearing witness with our spirit that we are children of God, and if children, then heirs, heirs of God and joint heirs with Christ, provided we suffer with Christ in order that we may also be glorified with Christ.

I consider that the sufferings of this present time are not worth comparing with the glory that is to be revealed to us. For the creation waits with eager longing for the revealing of the children of God; for the creation was subjected to futility, not of its own will but by the will of the one who subjected it in hope; because the creation itself will be set free from its bondage to decay and obtain the glorious liberty of the children of God. We know that the whole creation has been groaning in labor pangs together until now; and not only the creation, but we ourselves, who have the first fruits of the Spirit, groan inwardly as we wait for adoption, the redemption of our bodies. For in this hope we were saved. Now hope that is seen is not hope. For who hopes for what is seen? But if we hope for what we do not see, we wait for it with patience.

The Spirit helps us in our weakness; for we do not know how to pray as we ought, but that very Spirit intercedes for us with sighs too deep for words. And the one who searches human hearts knows what is the mind of the Spirit, because the Spirit intercedes for the saints according to the will of God.

We know that in everything God works for good with those who love God, who are called according to divine purpose. For those whom God foreknew God also predestined to be conformed to the image of the Son of God, in order that the Son might be the first-born among many children. And those whom God predestined God also called; and those whom God called God also justified; and those whom God justified God also glorified.

What then shall we say to this? If God is for us, who is against us? God did not spare God's own Son, but gave him up for us all; how shall God then not give us all things, along with the Son? Who shall bring any charge against God's elect? It is God who justifies; who is to condemn? Is it Christ Jesus, who died, yes, who was raised from the dead, who is at the right hand of God, who indeed intercedes for us?

Who shall separate us from the love of Christ? Shall tribulation, or distress, or persecution, or famine, or nakedness, or peril, or sword? As it is written,

'For your sake we are being killed
     all the day long;
we are regarded as sheep to be
     slaughtered.'

No, in all things we are more than conquerors through the one who loved us. For I am sure that neither death, nor life, nor angels, nor principalities, nor things present, nor things to come, nor powers, nor height, nor depth, nor anything else in all creation, will be able to separate us from the love of God in Christ Jesus our Lord.

> "You were anointed with exorcized oil and made partakers of the good olive tree, Jesus Christ."

CYRIL OF JERUSALEM

The ancient fable of the trees

The Book of Judges tells the story of Abimelech's short and nasty reign as the first king over an Israelite city. The historian clearly sided with Abimelech's youngest brother, Jotham, who rejected the very idea of a monarchy, seeing its hierarchical structure as troublesome in a tribal community. Jotham is credited with speaking out a poem in which the trees decide to anoint one tree king "to sway over them." The olive tree, however, rejects the request because it is too busy "producing rich oil by which gods and mortals are honored." The fig tree is too busy producing fruit, and the vine too busy producing wine. Only the useless bramble, which cannot provide even the shade so necessary in a sweltering climate, offers itself for the equally useless role of king.

Judges 9:7–15

I smile at what my tenth-grade English teacher called "the wide truths of life" in this ancient Mesopotamian poem. One bramble after another reigns in our lives, each as useless as the last, while the fig tree and the vine, our very food and drink, are sidelined. But let's attend to the olive tree, regarded in the ancient Near East as the noblest of trees. It provided the oil necessary to lubricate dry bodies, to treat wounds and sores, to cook up the family meal, and when *Exodus 28:41* spiced just right, to mark the people of highest religious and political *1 Samuel 10:1–2* significance. And I wonder: What is my olive oil? What do I see as that "by which gods and mortals are honored"? What is it that I live in, because it lives in me?

Paul's letter to the Romans

As we stand at the font, Romans 8 gives us a Christian answer. Baptism gives us the Spirit of Christ. That Spirit lives in us, and we live in that Spirit. We give it highest honor, and it honors us mortals. Paul uses several phrases to describe his hope: The Spirit of life is in us; we become children of God; we are connected to God by the love of Christ, beyond any possibility of separation. And the whole creation joins us. We're not talking here about humans being somehow eternally distinctive. No, the entire created order awaits the full and abundant life that the Spirit gives. Think of all those frogs, although declining in population, anticipating the life of God.

Cyril's lectures about baptism

Cyril was bishop of Jerusalem in the fourth century. With Christianity newly acceptable and even popular, with the emperor's mother Helena having scavenged Jerusalem for artifacts from the lifetime of Jesus, and with countless pilgrims following her example, the bishop of Jerusalem had his hands full of catechumens. He appears to have been a most capable teacher of the faith: We have his catechetical and mystagogical lectures, with their remarkable biblical knowledge, liturgical understanding and poetic genius refreshing us over the centuries. So what does Cyril say about the Spirit in baptism?

We are used to hearing that the oil anoints us all to be kings and queens, to be priests and prophets like the anointed ones of old. But Cyril reverses the image. We are not to reign, either over ourselves or over one another. Rather, we are to be filled with the oil of Jesus Christ the olive tree. Ah, brilliant metaphor, Cyril: for what is the olive tree, but the tree that rejected monarchy in order to be pressed out in service for others? The oil, says Cyril, symbolizes our participation in "the fatness of Christ," a richness that becomes our honor, not imaged as a monarch's crown but as a living tree producing its olives, providing for others that they might have life, life more abundantly. We are so dry, so dried up, that we need the oil from Christ the olive tree to anoint us back to life. Then, as the psalmist sings, we become "like a green olive tree in the house of God."

Psalms 52:8

Christ, the olive tree

Many different trees have been used to symbolize God's life. The eighteenth-century poet Joshua Smith called Christ the apple tree, "laden with fruit and always green." At Christmastime, the evergreen stands in our homes as a sign of Christ flourishing in the middle of winter. The dogwood's flower suggests to some people the cross with its traces of blood. The biblical images of the vine, the mustard bush and the cross itself are none of them even self-respecting trees, yet all paradoxically are trees of life.

John 15:1–11

Mark 4:31–32

For many poets, preachers and hymnwriters, Christ is the mythic
tree of life, bearing its twelve fruits, a tree as beyond nature as
our life in Christ is beyond our nature.

Revelation 22:1–2

But at baptism Christ is the olive tree. Our struggles with the
flood are finally over, we have been saved in the ark, and the
dove flies to us with an olive branch in its beak. It is as Paul wrote
to the Romans: the Spirit of God brings us Christ, the peace that
passes all understanding. The peace is achieved not by an aggressive
monarch, swaying over subjugated peoples, but by a nurse rubbing
oil on an aching body, a Good Samaritan pouring oil on our
wounds, a cook preparing the best possible meal with the finest
possible oil.

Genesis 8:6–11

Luke 10:29–37

And finally, Mecca salve

In my mother's midwestern hometown, the healing oil of choice for
the entire community was Mecca Salve. This heal-all was used
to anoint every possible bodily ache or sore, and its much-touted
miraculous powers always worked. All of us grown children
must now travel to Canada to stock up on Mecca, since the U.S.
Food and Drug Administration hasn't exactly recognized its poten-
tial to heal the nation. On the tube of Mecca as sold during my
childhood, the directions, incredibly, concluded with the line, "If
injury is serious, secure a larger jar." I remember getting a huge
sliver as a child: I anointed my arm with Mecca, and in the morning, the sliver was neatly lying on the bandage, the healing oils
having pulled it right out from under my skin while I slept. Mecca
was the oil in my family, and I still pack it in my suitcase.

Mecca Salve is my way to imagine olive oil. Baptism tells us
that Christ is the olive tree from which comes all healing oil,
and baptismal anointing makes us the source of oil in a world much

in need of soothing, healing and cooking. We see and feel the oil in a way difficult to see and feel the Spirit, who anoints us daily with baptismal life. So let us enjoy the anointing.

What is your oil, that by which you are honored?

How do you respond to the royal metaphor in the Bible and in the liturgy, the languge of Christ as King and of ourselves as reigning with him?

How much chrism should we use? When?

Imagine "the fatness of Christ."

O God,

olive tree for us,

nourishing our life, healing our bodies,

and pressed out for our joy,

anoint us, now and daily,

that we may live.

A WHITE ROBE

After this I looked, and lo, in heaven an open door! And the first voice, which I had heard speaking to me like a trumpet, said, "Come up hither, and I will show you what must take place after this." At once I was in the Spirit, and lo, a throne stood in heaven, with one seated on the throne! And the one who sat there appeared like jasper and carnelian, and round the throne was a rainbow that looked like an emerald. Round the throne were twenty-four thrones, and seated on the thrones were twenty-four elders, clad in white garments, with golden crowns upon their heads. From the throne issue flashes of lightning, and voices and peals of thunder, and before the throne burn seven torches of fire, which are the seven spirits of God; and before the throne there is as it were a sea of glass, like crystal.

And round the throne, on each side of the throne, are four living creatures, full of eyes in front and behind: the first living creature like a lion, the second living creature like an ox, the third living creature with a human face, and the fourth living creature like a flying eagle. And the four living creatures, each of them with six wings, are full of eyes all round and within, and day and night they never cease to sing,

"Holy, holy, holy, is the Lord
God Almighty,
who was and is and is to come!"

And whenever the living creatures give glory and honor and thanks to one who is seated on the throne, who lives for ever and ever, the twenty-four elders fall down before the one who is seated on the throne and worship the one who lives for ever and ever; they cast their crowns before the throne, singing,

"You are worthy, our Lord
and God,
to receive glory and honor
and power,
for you created all things,
and by your will they existed
and were created."

> "Christ is our clothing, who for love wraps us up, holds us close, entirely enclosing us for tender love."

JULIAN OF NORWICH

The state of clothes

I am one of those people for whom clothing is much connected to psychic state. Perhaps not many like me are left. But I wear great hats to church, a black dress to funerals, and tailored skirts to class. Not only do I don clothes to fit the occasion, but I know that to some extent the clothes don me. So it is that I do not think very well wearing an old sweatshirt, and I would not lecture with any authority wearing jeans.

Thus for me the biblical images of clothing are imaginally effective. There's Joseph's coat, much beloved in children's Bible story books for its many colors but now demoted by linguistic scholars to a "long robe with sleeves." Whichever, the robe was the symbol of devotion, as was the robe the father orders for the returning, ragged, prodigal son. The priest's robe, described in Exodus 39, included interwoven threads of hammered gold leaf and a breastplate inset with twelve precious and semi-precious stones, as well

Genesis 37:3

Exodus 39:1–21

as a hem lined with bells: no mail-order chasuble, this. But there's also the first death of anything living in the Genesis creation story: for animals had to die so that God could fashion leather clothing for Adam and Eve. But the clothing that has come to signify baptism is the white robe of the Revelation visions, worn first by the twenty-four elders seated around the throne of God and promised to us all, the great multitude beyond number.

Genesis 3:21

Why white?

The point of a white garment is not some interior purity, and surely not virginity, as recent wedding lore suggests. Modern white wedding dresses derive from the nineteenth-century court dress of European upper-class women, who wore white to prove that they were free from having to do any work and who wanted their outfit to stand out in a crowded room. The elaborate white wedding dress took hold in American society among the increasing number of women who would afford a new dress for the occasion, indeed an expensive dress that would be worn only once. The white of a wedding dress is clearly a social statement. But the white robe of Revelation's visions, far from being about one's self or one's income, is about wearing Christ, about being Christ's body in the world. Seeing us in our albs from across a crowded room, others recognize one of the baptized.

A hermit writing about clothes

A fourteenth-century mystic who wrote about clothing was Julian. We know little about her. Even her name is suspect, for since she lived as a solitary in a hut attached to St. Julian's church in Norwich, England, it is likely that she also abandoned her given name along with her other possessions when she decided to live at church. She had a series of visions upon which she meditated for 20 years before writing them down and interpreting their meaning.

How many outfits did she have in that hut? Two? Maybe three? I think of the cloak that Martin of Tours ripped in half, so that he could share his only coat with a poor man. I think of the robe of Francis of Assisi, now hanging in an airtight case, not the neat romanticized gown of Franciscans that one sees in movies, but shapeless sackcloth, much patched. Was Julian's robe like that?

In her Revelations she likens human nature to Adam's old tunic: "tight, bare and short," made dirty by hard, unhappy labor. To say that Christ joined us in human pain, Julian wrote that Christ donned Adam's tunic. We thus traded clothes with God. With divinity taking on our meager covering, we can take on the white robe of celebration, of release from work. This robe is fresh from the washtub, and it flows freely so that even our odd body shapes (am I too fat? too thin? hiding scars and wounds and deformities?) are covered over in gentle grace. It is as if we are returned to paradise, to a time before we had to labor for children and for food.

What did Julian have to keep herself warm? Some huge cloak? This woman, living quite alone, connecting with people always and only through a window, calls Christ her clothing, Christ "who for love wraps us up, holds us close, entirely enclosing us for tender love." With practically no clothes herself and with nobody's arms embracing her, she wrote in resonant serenity that "all shall be well, and all shall be well, and all manner of things shall be well." Covered as she was in the Trinity, she was richly attired, warmly dressed, lovingly robed.

Baptismal dress

So it is to be with our baptismal robe. Coming out of the font, the newly baptized put on white. Whether an infant's ruffled gown, adult street clothes or an alb, the white indicates that the baptized are newly free, free from the labor of Adam, free to don Christ and to walk about enwrapped in divine love. Unfortunately, some people have come to connect the white robe with ordination. No, the alb is baptismal garb, and when we see all the ministers and the whole choir circling around the altar at communion in their white robes, they are a picture of us all, circling around the throne of God at the end of time.

We don the robe and so are seen to be part of the body of Christ, a sign of divinity in this world weighed down by labor. But the robe dons us. One walks differently wearing an alb: no slouching around. When my daughters were old enough that they were no longer wiping their faces on my skirts, I bought a white dress: So it is with baptism. For while it is true that to be baptized is to get down on your hands and knees and scrub up the world's dirty floor, it is also true that baptism teaches us to walk with Julian's serenity, white robe flowing around our ankles, glowing in our baptism, experiencing what it means to be the image of God.

My grandmother said, "If you don't know what to wear in the morning, you've got too many clothes." How many clothes do you have?

What about wearing black for funerals?

Women in the Holiness churches like to wear white every Sunday. What are the pros and cons of dressing up for church?

In Japanese culture, white is the color of mourning. What color would be best for the albs of Japanese Christians?

We are dripping wet,

O God,

and nothing in our overloaded closets will do.

Give us your own clothing.

Clothe us, your body in the world,

with your mercy.

THE GARDEN IN PARADISE

REVELATION 22:1 – 5

Then the angel showed me the river of the water of life, bright as crystal, flowing from the throne of God and of the Lamb through the middle of the street of the city; also, on either side of the river, the tree of life with its twelve kinds of fruit, yielding its fruit each month; and the leaves of the tree were for the healing of the nations. There shall no more be anything accursed, but the throne of God and of the Lamb shall be in it, and the servants of God shall do homage; they shall see God's face, and on their foreheads shall be God's name. And night shall be no more; they need no light of lamp or sun, for the Lord God will be their light, and they shall reign for ever and ever.

> "I went into the garden before Prime. I was charmed by the clear water and flowing streams and fresh green of the surrounding trees. I asked myself what more was needed to complete my happiness in a place that seemed to me so perfect, and I reflected that it was the presence of a friend, intimate, affectionate, wise and companionable, to share my solitude."

GERTRUDE OF HELFTA

Kurt's gardens

My brother Kurt is a landscape gardener. His gardens are much-loved by the community, and his favorite, with its forty varieties of shrubs and flowers, was once featured in a glossy garden magazine.

He creates all-season gardens vibrant with textures of leaf and shades of color. One is amazed that shrubs come in so many different tones of green and grey and blue and gold.

Besides his own gardens, Kurt tends plots of public land, strips along roadways or patches in front of town buildings, spending his own money to purchase interesting miniature trees or ground cover. And here's why: As a Jehovah's Witness, he believes that when God comes at the end of this age, this world will be transformed into a garden for a perfect life here. Kurt regards his work as beginning the earth's transformation into the garden of God.

Other gardens

Not only Jehovah's Witnesses but Shakers, too, viewed the garden with its tree of life as a central symbol of the reign of God. The Amish, for whom the Garden of Eden story is significant, must be employed within a farm economy because they view the garden imagery as essential for their self-identity. Indeed, the whole of the Christian church, along with other of the world's religions, uses the garden image as one way to picture life with God. The garden as a place of peaceful growth, of complementary variety, of the serene cycle of death and life, is naturally symbolic of a world better than the one we see as we drive to work.

It's not surprising, then, that one of the images associated with baptism is the garden. Some early fonts, built as small in-ground pools, were covered with stone baldachins held aloft by pillars resembling trees, as if entering the font is entering the garden of God. Some of the church's teachers likened the period of mystagogy to a walk in a garden, a time to enjoy the richness of the resurrection and learn more about God's gifts. The great eighteenth-century hymn-writer Isaac Watts wrote that

We are a garden walled around,
Chosen and made peculiar ground;
A litle spot inclosed by grace
Out of the world's wild wilderness.

For the 50 days of Easter, indeed for the rest of our lives, our walk in the garden is delightful instruction in growth in God.

A garden deepened

But as with all other images, a garden is finally not big enough to contain baptism fully. Despite the Christian popularity of garden imagery, the scriptures do not present a simple garden as the final paradise. Rather, the garden gets superimposed on the city. In the great vision of Revelation 22, the tree of life—or is it two? the Greek is confusing, with one tree on both sides of the river—and the streams of flowing water are in the midst of the city with its gates and streets. We don't go back to Eden. We go on to Zion, the city transformed by the garden.

Revelation 22:2

Ezekiel 47:1–12

Revelation 21:1

Yet another variation is the gardens we associate with the life of Jesus. Only the gospel of John (wouldn't you know it! John is always one step beyond the others) calls the place of Jesus' betrayal a garden and the location of Jesus' tomb a garden. Some gardens! But of course this paradoxical imagery supports John's thesis that the place of Jesus' death is the place sprouting with life for us.

John 18:1

John 19:41

Gertrude's garden

We have from a thirteenth-century nun another variation on the garden image. Gertrude of Helfta grew up in a convent but at age 25 had a conversion experience. She is honored for the mystical visions which came to her during the community's daily office. We encounter her sitting in the convent's garden. Many monastic properties included a central garden radiating around a fountain and enclosed with a cloister, the differently carved pillars of which were meant to depict many varieties of trees in the garden of God. Gertrude is in such a cloister, after Prime, the time of the resurrection, and as if the garden is the baptized life, she delights in its flowing waters and vibrant greenery.

However, as a baptized Christian Gertrude knows that she and the garden are not enough. She in her garden requires "the presence of a friend, intimate, affectionate, wise and companionable, to share my solitude." The garden alone is no Christian garden. And who is the desired companion? Sometimes the very presence of God, sometimes a fellow nun, sometimes the kitchen maid, sometimes a stranger. The language from the Song of Songs of lover meeting lover in a garden reminds us that our days of mystagogy are not to be lonely ones, me sitting alone in a garden with my Bible or prayerbook. Rather, we in our garden have each other, the scriptures, indeed, the whole Christian community past and present, together discovering all 40 varieties of trees surrounding us.

And what a crowd!

So who's here with us in this baptismal garden? Nicodemus, the Samaritan woman, the man born blind, Lazarus, Martha and Mary hail from the ancient past. Peter, John and Paul are discussing the paschal mystery, and the visionary on Patmos and Perpetua herself are comparing visions. Under one tree I see a gang from the fourth century: Ambrose and Augustine, Zeno and Cyril of Jerusalem, Chrysostom and Gregory. From Alexandria comes the other Cyril, disputing theology. From the middle ages, from its convents and huts and city squares, we hear women's voices, Marguerite and Gertrude, Julian and Catherine. It's a great company, Gertrude. You are not alone in your garden.

And such conversation I overhear! Which is more true, that we are in the image of God, or that we are hiding behind the bushes? Do we live with the strength of the cross, or under the power of the demons? Can one enter into the mother's womb a second time and be born? Some of us have questions, some have answers. And that bishops' conference from the fourth century, they knew lots about baptism, but they sure have lots to learn about women. And here's another debate: Are we to be down on hands and knees washing someone's feet, or are we to be dancing around the table in white robes?

Plato proposed that what the immortality of the soul meant was that after death and into eternity great minds would sit around banquet tables in the skies and discuss such issues as truth and morality. Whether or not such a future is before us, such a present is already here. We are in the garden, sitting at a banquet table, discussing with both affectionate care and furious intensity what the baptized life ought to be. We learn from one another and correct one another, while singing together the Easter alleluia.

Come into the garden, and stay. Stay as long as you can. Stay until I am dead. Stay until you are dead. Stay until Easter is over.

Is there anyone who cannot be in the garden?

What's the climate in the garden of God? Why do you think so?

Why is it, do you think, that the visions in Revelation describe God as residing in a city?

Could Christians live out their baptismal life together "in a garden," or are we called to "the city"?

Be our garden,

O luxuriant and beauteous God.

May your flowers and fruits and every gracious green

enliven us in city and cemetery,

that together we may live together

through Christ, the living one.

ACKNOWLEDGMENTS

John Chrysostom, homily 26, in *Baptism: Ancient Liturgies and Patristic Texts*, ed. Andre Hamman, OFM (Staten Island NY: Alba House, 1967), 184.

The Ambrosian rite, in *Documents of the Baptismal Liturgy*, ed. E. C. Whitaker (London: SPCK, 1960), 139.

Catherine of Siena, prayer 10, in *The Prayers of Catherine of Siena*, ed. Suzanne Noffke, OP (New York: Paulist, 1983), 82.

The Gallican rite, in *Documents of the Baptismal Liturgy*, 160.

Perpetua, "The Martyrdom of Saints Perpetua and Felicitas," in *Maenads, Martyrs, Matrons, Monastics: A Sourcebook on Women's Religions in the Greco-Roman World*, ed. Ross S. Kraemer (Philadelphia: Fortress, 1988), 98.

Zeno, "Seven Invitations to the Baptismal Font," in *Baptism: Ancient Liturgies and Patristic Texts*, 65.

Marguerite d'Oingt, "The Mirror," in *Medieval Women's Visionary Literature*, ed. Elizabeth Alvilda Petroff (New York: Oxford, 1986), 292.

Ambrose, "The Sacraments," chapter 3, in *Saint Ambrose: Theological and Dogmatic Works*, tr. Roy J. Deferrari (Washington DC: Catholic University of America Press, 1963), 295.

Augustine, "The Three Whom Jesus Raised to Life," in *The Sunday Sermons of the Great Fathers*, tr. and ed. M. F. Toal (Chicago: Henry Regnery, 1959), IV, 119.

Cyril of Alexandria, "Meditation on the Mystical Supper and the Washing of the Feet," in *The Sunday Sermons of the Great Fathers*, III, 158.

Gregory of Nyssa, "A Sermon for the Feast of Lights," in *Baptism: Ancient Liturgies and Patristic Texts*, 132.

Cyril of Jerusalem, Mystagogical Catechesis II:3, in *Lectures on the Christian Sacraments*, ed. F. L. Cross (Crestwood NY: St. Vladimir's Seminary Press, 1977), 60.

Julian of Norwich, chapter 5, *Revelations of Divine Love*, ed. M. L. del Mastro (Garden City NY: Image Doubleday, 1977), 88.

Gertrude of Helfta, book 2:3, in *The Herald of Divine Love*, tr. and ed. Margaret Winkworth (New York: Paulist, 1993), 97.